Peter Neumann

CU00313248

Renate Daniel

THE SELF
Quest for Meaning in a Changing World

The Self

Quest for Meaning in a Changing World

by

Renate Daniel

DAIMON
Verlag

This book consists of a licensed translation and reworking of the original German edition, *Das Selbst, Grundlagen und Implikationen eines zentralen Konzepts der Analytischen Psychologie*, © 2018 Verlag W. Kohlhammer GmbH, Stuttgart.

This English-language version was rendered by Sibylle Pot d'or, assisted by Julia Czekierska.

The author and the publisher are grateful to the Susan Bach Foundation, Zurich, and the Stefanie + Wolfgang Baumann Foundation, Basel, for their generous financial support in support of the translation and publication of this project.

Cover illustration: A fractal flame rendered with the program Apophysis. Courtesy Jonathan Zander / Wikipedia.

Photograph of the author © Michael Seitter.

First edition 2020

Copyright © 2020 Daimon Verlag, Einsiedeln

ISBN 978-3-85630-781-3

All rights reserved.

For Trudel and Cyriak

Contents

About the author

Renate Daniel, MD, studied medicine at the University of Heidelberg before training as a specialist in psychiatry and psychotherapy at the Kehl-Kork Epilepsy Centre and the Emmendingen Centre for Psychiatry. At the same time, she received further training in psychoanalysis at the C.G. Jung Institute Zurich.

She currently has her own practice in Zurich and, as Director of Programs at the C.G. Jung Institute Zurich, is responsible for the organization of the semester program, as well as for numerous other issues in the operational management of the Institute.

For many years, she has been a lecturer, teaching analyst and supervisor at the C.G. Jung Institute Zurich, as well as actively teaching at the Jung Societies in Basel, Cologne and Stuttgart. She also participates as a course lecturer in the annual Lindau Psychotherapy Weeks held in Germany.

Foreword

It is a pleasure to provide the foreword to this book series. Looking back at the psychotherapeutic landscape from where we stand today, it might almost appear strange that there was a time when members of different "schools" argued vehemently about who was more successful, who had the better concept, who belonged to the mainstream, who did not, and who was of significant importance precisely because they did not belong. Meanwhile, we know from studies on psychotherapy that general factors – such as the nature of the therapeutic relationship, combined with the expectation of improvement, a patient's inner resources, and the environment in which individuals live and are treated – play a greater role than different treatment techniques. As research studies have shown (Practical Study on Outpatient Psychotherapy (PAPs) Switzerland), therapists nowadays use many general intervention techniques in addition to the school-specific ones, but above all, they use many approaches from disciplines other than those in which they were primarily trained.

Yet, precisely because we therapists have so much in common and we are unbiased when it comes to adopting intervention techniques from other disciplines, interest is growing in what the concepts of the "respective others" really are. As a Jungian, I notice time and again that Jung's theories are used as a "quarry", whose boulders then appear in a new construction style, or in a new "setting", without any reference to Jung. One example is Jungian dream interpretation, many aspects of which have been adopted whenever dream work is practiced today. The fact that C.G. Jung himself was not the first to work intensively with imagination, but that imagination is central to Jungian theory, has occasionally been "forgotten"; schema theory certainly cannot hide its proximity to Jungian complex theory, which emerged 100 years earlier.

Many conceptual overlaps may exist because Jung's original ideas are not known well enough. It is for this reason that I welcome Ralf Vogel's idea to publish a series of books, in which fundamental Jungian concepts – and their development – are described and formulated as we know them today, with a view to combining theory and practical work. I am certain that Jungian theory, in which imagery and the pictorial realm have such a great significance, can also serve as a source of inspiration for colleagues from other disciplines.

Verena Kast

Introduction

Although we use the term "self" in everyday parlance, as e.g. in self-confidence, self-assurance or self-doubt, it is difficult to explain what is meant. Similarly, the word "ego" is not easy to define, nor is the difference between the two terms "self" and "ego". Apparently, we cannot simply exchange "self" and "ego" at will, as we do not speak of ego-confidence or ego-healing, but of self-confidence or self-healing. Ego-consciousness and self-consciousness are not the same thing either. There is a difference between the ego and the self, which is what this book is all about.

For a psychologist, this difference is both interesting and relevant. Various schools of psychology define the terms "ego" and "self" in partially similar, but also different ways, and misunderstandings can easily arise if the respective definitions are not clarified. We ourselves often choose the most plausible psychological concept; sometimes we mix concepts, not always consciously, and occasionally, consensus on the prerogative of interpretation is lacking.

The aim of this book is not to find the most convincing self-concept, but to present C.G. Jung's core ideas about the ego and the self and examine their relevance in an everyday context.

Dealing with Jung's concept of the self means dealing with his concept of humanity and his ideas about God, the divine and the question of faith. For Jung, there was good reason to look at these topics from a psychological perspective, because they have always been of concern to us, and potential answers have a considerable impact on the way we shape our lives and relationships. These topics also influence ethical stances, ideologies, social and political processes and therapeutic models.

Jung's ideas and claims about the ego and the self are sometimes difficult to grasp or may appear contradictory. Some inconsistencies can be explained by his decades of "work in progress", during which he reconstructed and adapted his theory based on new insight and experience. However, paradox, vagueness and ambiguity are essential elements to a concept of the self, because associated statements are at least partly beyond our imagination and beyond rational logic. People might be irritated because religious questions touch upon what is venerable and "holy" to them. Across cultures and epochs, people have always been outraged whenever the "sacred" was called into question. It is almost impossible to remain calm when one's most preciously held concepts are disrespected by others. On that note, this book may well provoke, challenge or even annoy the reader – at least occasionally.

It would be helpful if you, as readers, were to engage with the ideas described herein as far as possible and without prejudice. My aim is not to convince you of Jung's concepts, but rather to contribute to a more conscious understanding of your own ideas and convictions in this regard, and the way these impact upon your self-image and world view.

Among the various approaches to the theme of "ego and self" available, I prefer the narrative described by philosopher Odo Marquard:

For human beings are their stories. But stories have to be told. This is what the human sciences do: They compensate for the damage done by modernization by telling stories. And the more things are objectified, the more, in compensation, stories have to be told: Otherwise humans die of narrative atrophy. (Marquard 1991, 98)

Significant narratives, such as myths, fairy tales, religion and literature, touch upon meaningful questions by addressing fundamental issues of human existence. As symbolic texts, however, they cannot be fully grasped and will at least to some extent defy comprehension. Hence, what is said and experienced remains provisional and mostly without scientific proof. The reader should therefore keep an open mind, both as far as the topic itself is concerned and the way it is presented in this book.

1. C.G. Jung's Concept of Ego and Self

Ego, Ego-Consciousness and Ego-Complex
in C.G. Jung's Teachings

Let's look at how C.G. Jung tries to define and describe the ego:

> Despite the unlimited extent of its bases, the ego is never more and never less than consciousness as a whole. As a conscious factor the ego could, theoretically at least, be described completely. But this would never amount to more than a picture of the *conscious personality;* all those features which are unknown or unconscious to the subject would be missing. A total picture would have to include these. (Jung 1959, CW 9/2, §7)

According to Jung, ego and consciousness represent abilities that are identical to knowledge, recognition and understanding. We have now named some central aspects of consciousness, but the exact makeup of consciousness and how it functions have yet to be clarified. Neurobiologist Antonio Damasio (Damasio 2000, 8) seriously doubts whether the cognitive sciences will ever be able to understand

and explain "consciousness" as a phenomenon. Despite this difficulty in understanding, we cannot avoid using the term "consciousness".

While consciousness represents our general ability to acquire knowledge of the world and skills, ego-consciousness enables us to recognize ourselves. This self-awareness is not yet present at birth, it gradually develops and becomes increasingly differentiated in a stepwise process. Around the age of two, ego-consciousness starts to emerge. Toddlers no longer speak of themselves in the third person, i.e. no longer say, "Sarah wants a cookie", but declare "I want a cookie".

Adults occasionally experience the emerging character of ego-consciousness on awakening. For a split second, we are not clear where we are or what day it is. Only the awakened, conscious ego is able to orient itself spatially, temporally and in relation to its self. It is very rare that healthy persons question who they are in the initial moments of waking up in the morning. Marc Wittmann (Wittmann 2018, 7f.) once experienced this firsthand. It did not take long for his memory to return, however, and along with it the certainty of his ego, the certainty of "being and existing as himself". Our ability to remember is thus a prerequisite for ego-consciousness, and in fact we cannot consciously remember experiences from the entire pre-ego period of early childhood. Conscious memories only become possible once the ego has been formed, but at the same time, memories lay the foundation of the ego. Without autobiographical memory, we do not know who we are, how the ego is structured and how it is embedded in the world. The ego becomes conscious of itself as soon as we become aware of our own stories, i.e. a narrative of our ego becomes accessible to us.

But the matter is not quite so simple. Damasio (Damasio 2000, 82ff) describes different levels of ego-consciousness, stating that our expanded ego-consciousness requires a wide range of cognitive abilities, such as attention, concentration, contemplation, etc. Most notably, learning and remembering enable an expanded ego-consciousness to enter into complex interactions with itself and the world. Damasio holds that before any cognition and memory of one's self as a person, and therefore before any learning experience has been gained, there exists a so-called core self, namely a feeling of being present, a perception of the ego or being a self.

As long as this core consciousness is intact, says Damasio, people experience emotions, which are inextricably linked to the primary core consciousness. The German title of his book therefore translates to *I feel, hence I am*, which ties in with Jung's concept of the ego as a complex:

> By ego I understand a complex of ideas which constitutes the centre of my field of consciousness and appears to possess a high degree of continuity and identity. Hence I also speak of an *ego-complex*. [...] for a psychic element is conscious to me only in so far as it is related to my ego-complex. [...] being merely one complex among other complexes. (Jung 1971, CW 6, §706)

The Latin root of the word complex is "to encompass", "to intertwine" and "to complete", indicating that each complex is a relatively self-contained whole and consists of several interwoven components. A complex includes all relationship experiences and notions related to the topic of the complex that have been stored in the memory. In connection with the ego complex, these would be experiences, images, thoughts, convictions or perceptions relating to the own ego, which are inseparably linked to feelings, or rather a whole array of feelings. They show that the ego complex is not a purely mental, but a physically anchored phenomenon of consciousness, because feelings are always psychosomatic and are experienced at the physical level. Metaphorical expressions, such as "having butterflies in one's stomach" or "a lump in one's throat", remind us of this connection. For this reason, the core consciousness of the ego described by Damasio must be rooted in the body, as referred to in the title of his book : The Feeling of What Happens. Body and Emotion in the Making of Consciousness. Damasio agrees with Jung that without a body, there is neither consciousness nor ego-consciousness. This physical reference is described by Jung as follows:

> The ego-complex in a normal person is the highest psychic authority. By this we mean the whole mass of ideas pertaining to the ego, which we think of as being accompanied by the powerful and ever-present feeling-tone of our own body. (Jung 1960, CW 3, §82)

The ego-complex is thus a psychosomatic phenomenon in which emotions play a crucial role. They are not always conscious, either because they are repressed or because they are part of an unconscious or semi-conscious background activity. Therefore, the ego-complex is more than our ego-consciousness, and, in my opinion, never fully conscious. Ego-consciousness as the center of the ego-complex, however, can draw attention to these emotions, to anything that has been forgotten or repressed, and make them largely conscious.

Ego-consciousness enables people to recognize their own reflection. This ability is not trivial, but rather an evolutionary advantage, because apart from chimpanzees and dolphins, animals cannot relate to their mirror image, and react by showing disinterest, flight or attack (cf. Roth 2001, 330). What happens on the psychological level when we look at ourselves in the mirror? What does this ability teach us about the nature of ego-consciousness? In front of the mirror, we divide ourselves into the observer and the observable, and are thus simultaneously subject and object, as Thomas Bernhard points out in his narrative "Walking":

> If we observe ourselves, we are never observing ourselves, but someone else. Thus, we can never talk about self-observation, or when we talk about the fact that we observe ourselves we are talking as someone we never are when we are not observing ourselves, and thus when we observe ourselves we are never observing the person we intended to observe but someone else. (Bernhard 2003, 74)

Ego-consciousness is thus an act of separation, which is why ego-consciousness and ego-being or being oneself are not the same thing. In the Japanese language, this is clearly evident, because "to recognize" also means "to be divided". The difference that is at stake is comparable to the difference between being a witness and being the one affected. Hence, ego-consciousness also implies that we can recognize our ability to be conscious and reflect on it – which would not be possible without language. Language and concepts are a prerequisite for gaining awareness.

We recognize ourselves in front of the mirror because of the distance between ourselves and the mirror. Ego-awareness requires distance and grants distance. However, we do not merely have to stand in front of the mirror to learn something about ourselves, we can also look at ourselves from a psychological perspective. For example, when we are angry, we may ask ourselves what is going on inside of us at the moment, and consciously observe an angry part of our personality from a certain distance. Distancing ourselves has the advantage that we are not constantly or completely at the mercy of emotions. When the ego-consciousness recognizes anger, there is no need for a destructive impulse to gain the upper hand and overwhelm the ego like a sort of natural disaster.

So at least the conscious ego occasionally gets to decide what it wants to do in the face of irrepressible anger. It is ego-consciousness that makes such considerations possible, and it is the prerequisite for such subjectively felt freedom:

> [...] despite the causal nexus man does enjoy a feeling of freedom, which is identical with autonomy of consciousness. [...] The existence of ego consciousness has meaning only if it is free and autonomous. (Jung 1958, CW 11, §391)

and

> The ego [...] Inside the field of consciousness it has, as we say, free will. (Jung 1959, CW 9/2, §9)

From a neurobiological point of view (Solms and Turnbull, 2004, 292), so-called free will shows itself, above all, in the ability to refrain from doing something. According to current knowledge, our free will, whose physical correlates are located in the prefrontal lobes, enables us to inhibit instincts or emotions. The ego thus proves that it can tolerate frustration, and has a sense of relatedness and discipline. This free will of the ego is the basis or prerequisite for human culture, because it facilitates increasing liberation from natural constraints. While wild animals are still invariably at the mercy of the laws of nature, the ego has won more and more inner and outer latitude through free will.

The Self in C.G. Jung's Teachings

Jung claims that from a psychological point of view, man consists of the conscious and the unconscious, using the concept of the self to refer to the sum of these two parts:

> I have suggested calling the total personality which, though present, cannot be fully known, the *self*. (Jung 1959, CW 9/2, §9)

and

> When we now speak of man, we mean the indefinable whole of him, an ineffable totality, which can only be formulated symbolically. I have chosen the term "self" to designate the totality of man, the sum total of his conscious and unconscious contents. (Jung 1959, CW 11, §140)

Jung proposes that we can neither know exactly nor can we put into words how or who we actually are. With our cognitive faculty, i.e. our ego-consciousness, we encounter substantial limitations in this respect, because the unconscious can never become fully conscious. Since something always remains hidden, it is extremely difficult to say anything precise about the self from a Jungian point of view. The self as a complex personality is, so to speak, beyond our grasp, and can only be approximated on a more general level. Literature professor Peter von Matt speaks of the "primordial human mystery" (von Matt 2003, 58) to illustrate this ambiguity and opaqueness. We know that we are, but not exactly what and who we are. In his opinion, the mind cannot solve this riddle and poetry is needed to this end. He refers to Angelus Silesius, a theologian, physician and mystic of the 17th century, who speaks of the ego, but actually describes the self as C.G. Jung would have done:

I know not what I am; I am not what I know;
A thing and not a thing, a point and circle's flow.

The center of the circle is the exact point where the compass is inserted. As a point, it is a mathematical void, a place without extension. At the same time, this tiny hole is of central importance as the birthplace and center of the circle. The poem creates a tension between the experience of nothingness (mathematically) and importance (the center of the circle). Many people are familiar with this tension from their self-esteem experience which can oscillate from a feeling of absolute worthlessness (the individual as a tiny cog) to self-elevation or overestimation of one's own capabilities (nothing is impossible). In his *Critique of Practical Reason*, Immanuel Kant defines this tension of opposites as follows:

> Two things fill the mind with ever new and increasing admiration and reverence, the more often and more steadily one reflects on them: the starry heavens above me and the moral law within me. [...] The first view of a countless multitude of worlds annihilates, as it were, my importance as an animal creature [...] The second, on the contrary, infinitely raises my worth as an intelligence by my personality, in which the moral law reveals to me a life independent of animality and even of the whole sensible world. (Kant 2015, 129)

For Kant, the capacity for morality and ethics is the key value against which human meaning and value can be measured, which is reminiscent of the aforementioned neurobiological definition of free will.

19

The Paradox of the Self

Jung describes two aspects of the self: the self as a whole personality, on the one hand, and the self as the center of our whole personality on the other, which is difficult to understand on a rational level. The self may therefore be experienced simultaneously in two fundamentally different ways: as a totality encompassing the ego, or as an unconscious center of personality, which as an inner central point relates to a weaker ego-consciousness or the ego-complex:

> [...] if we conceive of the ego as being subordinated to, or contained in, a supraordinate self as centre of the total, illimitable, and indefinable psychic personality. (Jung 1958, CW 11, §67)

At the same time, the ego and the self are interwoven and the quality of their relationship remains elusive:

> However one may define the self, it is always something other than the ego, [...] the self is a more comprehensive thing which includes the experience of the ego and therefore transcends it. Just as the ego is a certain experience I have of myself, so is the self an experience of my ego. It is, however, no longer experienced in the form of a broader or higher ego, but in the form of a non-ego. (Jung 1958, CW 11, §885)

The author Janne Teller has encountered this phenomenon in her writing. Her words flow from a source, which cannot be identified as the ego, and it is not clear who is contained in whom:

> [...] when I write. Then Everything is connected, then I know Everything, because then I am not me, but a part of this Everything, and it is Everything that finds the words.

[...] Everything is not a state in which one can move freely. [...] Nor can one say that one knows Everything, because after all, things are at the same time what they cannot be. It is simply as if Everything were a part of oneself, or perhaps the other way around, that one is part of Everything and can therefore tap into its knowledge. [...] You can't talk about Everything without Everything disappearing. [...] Everything may not be in the fingers, but it can flow through them. Everything may not be at your fingertips, but it can flow through them. (Teller 2013, 128ff*[1])

and

Everything is like an endless lake of universal humanity. Everything is the lake I tap into when I write. (Teller 2013, 141f*)

Janne Teller's "Everything" reaches far beyond the personal ego and the personal unconscious. It belongs to all humankind and is shared by everyone. In this context, Analytical Psychology refers to the collective unconscious – a layer in the unconscious to which all humanity contributes – with the self as its center. Hence, the self would not be of an exclusively individual, but also of a transpersonal, collective nature, which Angelus Silesius terms as follows:

God is my center when I close him in; And my circumference when I melt in him. (after Jung 1970, CW 14/1, §128, footnote 70)

The reason why I am able to refer to this wording by Silesius and also to the statement by Paul the Apostle: "He is in you and you in him", is because Jung makes a quantum leap in further statements about the self by equating it

---

1. References marked with * have been translated from the German original.

with our inner-soul image of God, which some may consider provocative:

> Psychology, as I have said, is not in a position to make metaphysical statements. It can only establish that the symbolism of psychic wholeness coincides with the God-image, but it can never prove that the God-image is God himself, or that the self takes the place of God. (Jung 1959, CW 9/2, §308)

and

> Intellectually the self is no more than a psychological concept, a construct that serves to express an unknowable essence which we cannot grasp as such, since by definition it transcends our powers of comprehension. It might equally well be called the "God within us." The beginnings of our whole psychic life seem to be inextricably rooted in this point, and all our highest and ultimate purposes seem to be striving towards it. [...] I hope it has become sufficiently clear to the attentive reader that the self has as much to do with the ego as the sun with the earth. They are not interchangeable. Nor does it imply a deification of man or a dethronement of God. [...] When, therefore we make use of the concept of a God we are simply formulating a definite psychological fact, namely the independence and sovereignty of certain psychic contents which express themselves by their power to thwart our will, to obsess our consciousness and to influence our moods and actions. (Jung 1966, CW 7, §399f)

and

> Unity and totality stand at the highest point on the scale of objective values because their symbols can no longer be

distinguished from the imago Dei. (Jung 1959, CW 9/2, §60)

As early as the 13th century, A.D., Sufi Master Dschalal ad-Dın Muhammad ar-Rumı postulated that God or the image of God is not to be sought outside, but rather inside of us:

> I tried to find Him on the Christian cross, but He was not there.
> I went to the Temple of the Hindus and to the old pagodas, but I could not find a trace of Him anywhere. I searched on the mountains and in the valleys, but neither in the heights nor in the depths was I able to find Him.
> I went to the Caaba in Mecca, but He was not there either.
> I questioned the scholars and philosophers, but He was beyond their understanding.
> I then looked into my heart and it was there where He dwelled that I saw Him. He was nowhere else to be found.

From a psychological perspective, contemplating the issue of inside or outside leads us to the phenomenon of projection, meaning that by shifting the unconscious part of our soul to the outside world, it becomes perceptible. That which is hidden in the human soul can unwittingly and unintentionally be projected onto an external object, which then accumulates characteristics not normally associated with it. When the term "rose-colored spectacles" is used in the vernacular to denote lovers, for example, it refers to the projectively clouded vision of those who have just fallen in love. People in love do not view each other realistically, but rather tend to see themselves in a too positive light and overestimate each other's qualities. What is read into the other person is a piece of one's own soul. The inner and outer worlds are thus intertwined: a part of the subject is seen in the object. And these perceptions or attributes come as a surprise to the rest of us who are not in love and not susceptible to such projections.

However, projectivity should not be confused with error. Admitting a common mistake after we have received new or additional information is not a problem for many of us. Adjusting our projections, on the other hand, is quite difficult because the crushing weight of reality can lead to disappointment, anger, crises in self-esteem or depression. While a projection binds us emotionally to a person, an ideology, a cause, a task, etc., the withdrawal of a projection leads to separation and loss, usually also accompanied by intense emotions. Trying to make someone who has just fallen in love aware that their projection onto a person is unrealistic often fails because of the affective power of the projection. Reason is too weak a tool to counter a person's faith in projection.

If the human capacity for projection were to include the self, the image of God would be a construction of the human mind dependent on the zeitgeist. Psychologically, then, a distinction must be made between images of God, e.g. as a possible divine spiritual core in humans as described by Silesius and Rumi, and the existence of an independent God. Images of God can be researched and talked about, but God himself far less so, because many believe that God is beyond all spatial category of thought; this is formulated in Jewish mysticism as follows: "If one speaks of God, one speaks, oh, no longer of God" (Röser 2014, 130 *).

For Jung, the shape of the self as a personality center is also a divine authority of the unconscious, a divine will or God's voice (Jung 1959, CW 9/2, §49). As a rule, this voice can be clearly distinguished from the voice of reason, which belongs to ego-consciousness and the ego-complex.

A 40-year-old female architect describes this inner experience as follows: "One morning over coffee a voice suddenly said to me: 'You'd be better off alone!' I was stunned. What on earth was this? Was I going crazy? But the voice was really there, sounding somehow warm-hearted but at the same time brutal, cold, and very clear. It sounded very much like my own voice and yet it was different. It was a very impressive, touching voice. A year later, the voice re-appeared out of nowhere and said: 'You shouldn't be doing that job.' If I talk about it now, it brings tears to my eyes. The voice shook me to the core. It was my voice, but it would be incorrect to say that I had actually uttered those words. I can't describe it in a better way." And when a retired civil servant heard a voice speak to him in a dream and say: "Now go and open that dusty basket-weave chest in the basement", he sensed that he finally had to face his past. He woke up with the impression that he had received this order from an authority higher than his ego.

Anyone who has heard such voices and has had to seriously grapple with them, has developed a religious attitude according to Analytical Psychology. Religiousness is understood in this context as being in relation to the self, as a careful observation of the self by the conscious ego. Jung writes about this relationship between the ego and the self:

> The ego is, by definition, subordinate to the self and is related to it like a part to the whole. [...] our free will [...] finds its limits [...] where it comes into conflict with the facts of the self. [...] It is, indeed, well known that the ego not only can do nothing against the self, but is sometimes actually assimilated by unconscious components of the personality that are in the process of development and is greatly altered by them. (Jung 1959, CW 9/2, §9)

His assertion of the relationship between a weaker ego and a more powerful self may evoke the unpleasant, perhaps even unacceptable idea of an inferior, weak ego.[2] But such a negative view would be one-sided. French pianist Lucas Debarque knows how the more powerful self can have an enriching and productive effect on the ego:

> Music is spiritual. It has to do with the soul. You have to be wide awake and be open to what is around you. It's not about the ego. I, for example, don't know what I want. I let it happen. I can't help it. I do what I have to do. (Debarque 2016 *)

Lucas Debarque describes how he tries to keep his ego alert to the influx of the unconscious, which he also experiences as inevitable. The real task of the ego is to absorb creative material, in his case music, and to shape it for himself and others. Creativity thus draws from a source in the collective unconscious, which Janne Teller has described in a very similar way. Scientists also know this phenomenon. Chemist August Kekulé is said to have discovered the ring shape of the benzene molecule after a snake biting its tail appeared before his inner eye. Kekulé had already been thinking intensively about the structure of the benzene molecule and become stuck in the process when suddenly this inner image appeared to him while he was dozing. The breakthrough came only because his ego paid attention to this image and did not immediately reject it as nonsensical or irrelevant. Without ego-consciousness, the treasures of the unconscious would not be uncovered. The self needs the ego to be recognized and realized. Ultimately, the ego and the self need one another,

---

2. When German Federal President Frank Walter Steinmeier said the words "So help me God" upon being sworn into office in March 2017, a journalist reacted by stating that Steinmeier was imploring for help from above with this ancient formula, proving that he alone was too weak to be in office.

which actually makes the question of power obsolete, as Angelus Silesius puts it:

I am as great as God,
And he is small like me;
He cannot be above,
Nor I below him be.
(quoted from Jung 1967, CW 13, §151)

The images of God that have existed since time immemorial do not initially tell us anything about the possible existence of a God. According to physicist Wolfram Schommers (Schommers 1997, 498) and neurobiologists Solms and Turnbull (Solms and Turnbull 2004, 69), we cannot make any scientifically proven statement about fundamental reality, nor the existence or non-existence of God in principle, but have to content ourselves with images. And we basically do not know to what extent these images come close to the actual structures of fundamental reality. This basic assumption coincides with Jung's definition of the archetype and is of interest to us insofar as he considers the self to be the most important archetype of all (Jung 1959, CW 9/2, §422). Like any other archetype, the self per se is unimaginable, unknown and cannot be formulated, since it is part of fundamental reality. And like any archetype, the self can only be expressed more or less accurately through images, symbols and allegories. For the archetype of the self, these are mainly images of God in the various religious traditions. Psychologically speaking, such images and traditions are human projections. The actual self, like every archetype, lies unrecognizably hidden behind these projections. This in turn does not mean that people cannot have access to this reality by looking beyond the "border" through intuition, vision or experience.

Like the ego complex, the self is not a purely spiritual phenomenon, but includes our body:

> In Western psychology, the "self" stands for a totality which comprises instincts, physiological and semi-physiological phenomena. To us, a purely spiritual totality is inconceivable. (Jung 1958, CW 11, §808)

and

> Psychologically speaking, the domain of "gods" begins where consciousness leaves off, for at that point man is already at the mercy of the natural order, whether he thrive or perish. (Jung 1958, CW 11, §231)

The self as a whole personality also has a body, and the instincts and urges working from the unconscious are powerful forces. The ego finds it difficult to resist them, which becomes evident when we think of hunger, thirst, sexuality or sleep. Jung holds that natural urges and nature belong to the powers of God, and he does not rule out that the unconscious and God are one and the same:

> We cannot tell whether God and the unconscious are two different entities. (Jung 1958, CW 11, §757)

A conservative believer may find it disturbing to equate God with the unconscious, but whoever, like Jung (Jung 1959, CW 9/1, §261), understands religion as the living relationship of the conscious ego with the dark mental processes of the unconscious, will hardly take issue with this. Jung's concept and equation, i.e. the self = non-conceivable overall personality = image of God, can easily be confusing in linguistic terms. When we speak of self-confidence, self-awareness, self-recognition, self-assertion, etc. in everyday life, then by self we sometimes mean the ego, and very often our complete being, but rarely do we mean an image of God or something divine. This equation may indeed be troublesome, and we could of course argue that we are simply not conscious of all this. Interestingly, the Jewish scholar Friedrich Weinreb writes that experience of God is self-experience (Weinreb 2002, 34) and thus, like Jung, connects the two phenomena.

Symbols of the Self

In which images and symbols does the self then show itself?

[...] the self [...] its symbols range from the highest to the lowest. (Jung 1959, CW 9/2, §57)

This idea contradicts the notion of an exclusively good self. The self comprises not only of the good, the redeeming and the healing, but also of the most terrible thing imaginable. In this regard, Master Eckhart speaks of hell at the bottom of the human soul (von Franz 1978, 114).

Just how such extremes can come together is manifested in the dream an adult man had when he was 14, and which he recollects vividly (cf. Steiner 2003, 38): In his dream, he is standing in a completely destroyed city. All around him are rubble and bent metal. Next to him, small puddles of water reflect a rainbow in splendid colors. The dreamer falls into an ecstatic mood. Ecstasy is an uncontrollable phenomenon which cannot be commanded deliberately, it just happens. I therefore suspect that the dreamer had an arousing, invigorating experience of the self. The destroyed city and the rainbow could be opposite poles of the self, triggering intense emotions: fear, despair, but also a fascination that leads to ecstasy. In his dream, destruction is complemented by the most extreme contrast – a colorful rainbow, the sight of which delights many people. As a bridge between heaven and earth, in ancient times it was a symbol for the relationship between humans and God, between the ego and the self. One of the images that has been handed down is the rainbow that God placed in the sky after the Flood as a sign of His covenant with humankind. The patient's therapist notes that his inner world was dominated by hopelessness, despair and destroyed objects – an intolerable situation. In perceiving the dream in its entirety, something wonderful appears alongside the destruction. Even if it is difficult to engage in this irrational coexistence of the terrible and the wondrous, a dream such as this one can be an invitation to address this question. It is about cruelty and goodness not only in the outer world, but also in humans themselves. It questions how people can be capable of torturing others, whilst being loving in other situations. It deals with the riddle of the human abyss and destructiveness. This, too, is part of the self. Jung further describes the varied content of the symbols of the self:

> Moreover, the self is felt empirically not as subject but as object, and this by reason of its unconscious component, which can only come to consciousness indirectly, by way of projection. Because of its unconscious component the self is so far removed from the conscious mind that it can only be partially expressed by human figures; the other part of it has to be expressed by objective, abstract symbols. The human figures are father and son, mother and daughter, king and queen, god and goddess. Theriomorphic symbols are the dragon, snake, elephant, lion, bear, and other powerful animals, or again the spider, crab, butterfly, beetle, worm, etc. Plant symbols are generally flowers (lotus and rose). These lead on to geometrical figures like the circle, the sphere, the square, the quaternity,

the clock, the firmament, and so on. The indefinite extent of the unconscious component makes a comprehensive description of the human personality impossible.
(Jung 1959, CW 9/1, §315)

This enumeration could be confusing and difficult to understand in a logical way. How can we navigate through life when the self can apparently be projected onto all kinds of things? On human, animal, plant, abstract or inanimate figures, on the most valuable and total rubbish? Do we not run the risk of assuming the self behind everything and everyone? Quite certainly. And hence, as a rule, it is not the content of the image alone, but the associated emotional experience that indicates whether the self could be involved. Shock, amazement, fright or existential emotion are just some of the experiences that people describe when they have come into contact with the self, often connected with a subjective certainty of being touched by something greater, majestic or holy. Enthusiasm is also a state that comes close to the self, provided that its literal translation from the Greek, i.e. "being filled with God" or "being possessed by God" is taken seriously.

The Self as God the Father – the Ego as the Child of God

The fact that mother or father images can be projected onto the self is based on the idea that the ego develops out of the self:

> The self, like the unconscious, is an *a priori* existent out of which the ego evolves. It is, so to speak, an unconscious prefiguration of the ego. It is not I who create myself, rather I happen to myself. (Jung 1958, CW 11, §391)

31

This description considers ego-consciousness as a child of the unconscious, which becomes increasingly autonomous, but never completely independent, never completely free from the unconscious. The ego and the unconscious, as well as the ego and the self, remain related to each other throughout life, sometimes in extreme conflict, sometimes in more or less fruitful coexistence. If the unconscious is understood to be the parents of the ego, it is not surprising that in the course of human history, mother and father images have been projected onto the self. These images, however, "transcend" the human father and the human mother, becoming evident in the biblical God, who as a Father created humans in his own image and likeness.[3] The image of humans (ego) and the image of God (self) are therefore closely related, but at the same time very different, as illustrated, for example, by the omnipotence, omniscience, immortality or creative power of this God the Father. God may be close to humankind, but entirely different. And if we project this image of God the Father onto our human father or another person, then this person is endowed with superhuman qualities, is admired and worshipped – or excessively feared and hated. Such projections can be contagious and affect large groups of people or nations. As a result, more and more individuals start to project in a similar way and share the same views of reality, which then become officially recognized, for example, in the form of a state religion or ideology. The few remaining sceptics are quickly branded as heretics or traitors, only to be rehabilitated as pioneers at a later date, when these old ideas have been overcome and new ones established.

---

3. There is some dissent about the term "likeness". Instead of translating it with *likeness*, some translate the Hebrew term "Zelem" with *similarity*, others with *shadow image*. Humans would then be the shadow image of God. (Graf 2009, 87)

Those who, like Jung, see the self as divine can understand biblical texts as symbolic descriptions of inner-soul processes, which confront individuals not only from the outside, but also as a part of themselves. Genesis recounts the development of human consciousness and the birth of the ego. By eating from the tree of knowledge, humans learned to distinguish between good and evil. The Bible equates being human with the capacity to assess situations and deeds from a moral and ethical point of view. This had its consequences, though, and led to expulsion from paradise – conscious awareness does indeed have consequences. Humans are no longer harmoniously constrained by or embedded in the laws of nature, and the Bible describes the expulsion from paradise as a loss of natural innocence, referring to the more uncomfortable side of human consciousness. Since we can understand and assess the consequences of our actions, we are probably the only living beings who can be held responsible for our actions and, at the same time, are aware of this responsibility. Psychologically speaking, once we become aware of something, we are no longer innocent children. Under certain circumstances, this can be perceived as burdensome or even threatening, as the case of a 50-year-old patient in therapy illustrates. He criticized his therapist after she had encouraged him to reflect on his inner resources for the first time. His anger was rooted in the fact that he had been looking for someone to listen, to give him support and warmth, not someone who would encourage his self-perception and self-awareness. Something within him (still) resisted becoming conscious, threatening his feelings of security.

Since consciousness always entails becoming aware of differences, it leads to a severance of ties and independence. Some people may experience loneliness, lack of orientation or feel cast out in the process – and therefore try to avoid it.

People who have not experienced positive attachment can feel particularly overwhelmed.

Ego-consciousness needs a sustainable, readily responsible ego, which is why working on the ego is immensely important in a therapeutic setting. Without a strong ego, a conscious confrontation with the inner-soul and outer challenges cannot take place. If patients cannot overcome a strong (unconscious) longing for infantile dependence or security, their resistance to becoming conscious tends to be high, at least in the early stages of therapy.

From a neurobiological point of view, becoming conscious during psychotherapy amplifies the functional capacity of the prefrontal lobe. Imaging techniques have shown that functional changes brought about by psychotherapy are mainly localized in the prefrontal lobes (Solms and Turnbull 2004, 299).

The Bible mentions another consequence of human cognitive capacity, namely that humans becomes God-like. Jung and Weinreb postulated that becoming aware of oneself is like becoming aware of God, and becoming oneself is like becoming God. Hence, biblical images illustrate how the ego steadily increases its autonomy, competence and efficiency by means of this cognitive capacity. Smallness, powerlessness or helplessness in the ego can gradually be attenuated. In other words, abilities which were once associated with the self (image of God), and were denied humankind, have now become increasingly available to us. Greek mythology describes this as a kind of robbery, as exemplified by Prometheus stealing fire from the gods to bring it to the people. This fire is an important step towards reaching independence from divine powers.

In a biblical context, consciousness is not a gift. It was only because Adam and Eve disobeyed that they became conscious.

Hence, disobedience is the *conditio sine qua non* of human con-sciousness. Interestingly enough, the Bible's images of humans and God trace the accumulation of knowledge back to the breaking of taboos and the crossing of boundaries. According to Genesis, such behavior is part of human existence and to this day linked to the question of how far humankind, and thus the ego, may go. Genesis mentions the breaking of taboos without setting any limits, so that the fascinating prospect of becoming God-like appears on the horizon. From a psychological standpoint, the ego and the self would then be identical and harbor both developmental opportunities as well as risks. Jung believes that those who cease to believe in God are in danger of succumbing to inflation and thus, to an overestimation and exaggeration of their selves (Jung 1958, CW 11, §142).

The Development of the Self

Images of all archetypes, including the self, are not static or eternal, but rather of a fundamentally provisional nature, as von Franz notes:

> You know, archetypes have histories over the centuries. [...] archetypes constellate themselves, develop, age, bring up their opposite; there is a whole play that goes on over hundreds and hundreds of years. And you can say there are certain archetypes that recede. They have played a great role but then they fade. People lose interest in them. [...] They become forgotten. (von Franz 2000, 44)

and

> Religions, convictions, truth, they all age. Everything that has been talked about too much and which has for a while

ruled human society is deficient in the sense that it ages. It becomes mechanical, too well known, a possession of consciousness. People feel that by knowing about it they have it. And this affects the highest values most because smaller things do vary after a while and it doesn't matter. But if the highest values wear out, if they lose their shattering numinous quality, then naturally there is a great danger. And that's why, for instance, keeping taboos degenerates into simply keeping formalities without seeing any meaning in them. One is no longer moved by the myth which is behind every taboo. (von Franz 2000, 24)

Images of God emerge, or, one can also say, are brought forth, only to age and expire at some point. The ravages of time take their toll on the images of God, until one day "God is dead", as Friedrich Nietzsche put it. At this point, images of God become meaningless and like empty shells. They only remain relevant in a specific historical context, reminding us of what was once considered important. Today, for example, most people are no longer able to believe in God as a person, a white-bearded man sitting in heaven. This image of God has lost all impact and value. People for whom the image of God the Father in heaven does not mean very much, however, are not necessarily atheists. About two-thirds of the German nation believe that a higher order exists, or some sort of higher energy has an impact on life. Jung described this proclivity towards abstract imagery when pondering about what would happen if people could no longer project the traditional image of God:

> The experience formulated by the modern mandala is typical of people who cannot project the divine image any longer. Owing to the withdrawal and introjection of the image they are in danger of inflation and dissociation

of the personality. The round or square enclosures built round the centre therefore have the purpose of protective walls or of a *vas hermeticum*, to prevent an outburst or a disintegration. Thus the mandala denotes and assists exclusive concentration on the centre, the self. This is anything but egocentricity. On the contrary, it is a much needed self-control for the purpose of avoiding inflation and dissociation (Jung 1959, CW 11, §156).

In a way, Jung already stretched his feelers out into the 21st century when he predicted images of God would disappear and the stability of the ego complex be threatened by an initial vacuum. A look at the English bestseller list of a large online retailer reveals today's increasing need for the abstract structural order he described: In August 2015, there was a strong demand for adult coloring books with pre-printed mandalas. Scientists promote this kind of activity, saying that focusing on lines, boundaries and structures enhances brain function and concentration. Stress reduction aids could also indicate that more and more people are looking for a compensatory stabilization of the ego complex. Abstract geometric shapes, which have been found in religious representations since time immemorial, seem to satisfy this collective need.

Abstraction of the Image of God

Jung described the idea of God as a higher might or energy as follows:

> God would thus be not only the essence of spiritual light [...] but also the darkest, nethermost cause of Nature's blackest deeps. This is a tremendous paradox which obviously reflects a profound psychological truth. For it asserts

the essential contradictoriness of one and the same being, a being whose innermost nature is a tension of opposites. Science calls this "being" energy, for energy is like a living balance between opposites (Jung 1969, CW 8, §103)

and

> [...] the self is not just a static quantity or constant form, but is also a dynamic process. In the same way, the ancients saw the *imago Dei* in man not as a mere imprint, as a sort of lifeless, stereotyped impression, but as an active force. (Jung 1959, CW 9/2, §411)

There is an ancient and recurring idea of God as an invisible, omnipresent energy. In earlier cultures, this was referred to as Mana, Numinosum, Wakanda or Oki – to name but a few terms. Some of these do not denote energy alone, but also something sacred, powerful, creative, infinite or immortal. Earlier cultures took advantage of the fact that this energy is wholly unattached, but can be channeled almost anywhere by fasting, praying, dancing, touching holy objects or by using certain breathing techniques. In this way, we are able to appropriate part of this energy. From a psychological point of view, the ego complex can be enriched with energy that then becomes available for free will, awareness and cultural activities. The largest part of this energy of the soul, which Jung calls libido (Jung 1956, CW 5, §130ff), remains inaccessible in the unconscious and may only be perceived in the form of desires, urges, movements, emotions or interests.

Energy is a concept that transcends moral or aesthetic categories. The sun lends its energy to the just and the unjust, allowing both weeds and cultivated plants to grow. This characteristic of energy is taken up by the Old Testament in the image of Yahweh, who is known for his amorality. A God such as this, and therefore the self, is unpredictable.

2. Fate and the Self over the Course of Time

Diffusion of Responsibility

Images of the self are closely interlinked with questions of fate – everything that happens to us and is inevitable. In recent years, the scope of the inevitable has altered tremendously. A large number of options is now available to us, the consequences of which are difficult to keep track of. Hence, it is not always easy to make decisions, and when faced with forces beyond our control, it is helpful to clarify where human responsibility begins and where it ends.

This differentiation turned out to be essential for a woman who experienced grief and despair after the following dream: "I have given birth to a child, it is very small, it fits into the hollow of my hand. Its skin is so smooth that it keeps slipping out of my hand. It feels the cold, but because it is so small, I cannot wrap it in a cloth or dress it. I would like to breastfeed it, but this is impossible because my breasts are too big. The child is alive, which is nice. But it is shivering. It becomes cold, it dies."

For an unusually long time, the dreamer was tormented by these dream images and felt responsible for the infant's death.

Only once she realized she had done everything in her power did her feelings of guilt start to disappear, and she was able to accept the death of this tiny being as a fateful event. The guilt of the dreamer began to subside the very moment she ceased to assume an unreasonable level of accountability. On a subconscious level, she had attributed fate as belonging to the realm of human influence, and such megalomanic fantasies often lead to exaggerated feelings of guilt. If such diffusion of responsibility can be unscrambled, the ego's responsibility can be reduced to a more appropriate level, which will be higher in some situations and lower in others.

In ancient Greece, Homer's concept of fate attached great importance to this differentiation of responsibility. Back then, it was postulated that human and divine deeds were interwoven. Neither decisions nor deeds were entirely attributed to humans, since they were always surrounded by gods, from whom all significant events were believed to originate. The fact that human success was only possible with the help of the divine should not be forgotten, and the consequences of human failure had to borne by those at the cause of it. However, divine involvement meant a shared responsibility. Talent and luck, audacity and wisdom, as well as cowardice, incapacity and misfortune were all rooted in the divine. Even a brilliant idea was not a solely human product, it was the idea of a god gifted to humans. Still, these were at liberty to avail themselves of a good idea or chance, or to accept divine advice, but had to assume responsibility for whatever decisions they took.

From a psychological point of view, Greeks thus considered the self as a source of both destruction and grandeur. The mere capacity to differentiate transpersonal and individual influences made it possible for them to avoid an inappropriate level of self-depreciation or arrogance. Wisdom implied being able to live in relation to one's self and to differentiate the inaccessible from the controllable and feasible. Yet, this differentiation was never easy to achieve, since the transition between human and divine areas of responsibility were deemed fluid. This residual vagueness calls for careful respect for the self and the ego.

Concepts of Fate are Subject to the Zeitgeist

What is controllable, then, and how can we be prepared for what is to come? Jeremias Gotthelf's novella *The Black Spider*, published in 1842, illustrates the late medieval view on this subject: The plot evolves around an age-old black wooden Gothic window post. During a christening ceremony, a grandfather tells his guests the background to the story: 600 years ago, the village belonged to a knight who mercilessly forced his peasants to do the hardest work. One day, he demands that they replant one hundred fully grown beeches. The peasants are well aware that they cannot fulfill this task without neglecting their work in the fields and suffering a famine as a consequence. In this hopeless situation, the devil appears in the shape of a wild-looking hunter and offers his help. As a reward, he demands an unchristened child. The shocked peasants reject his offer and pray for God's help instead – in vain, as God does not show himself. He does not intercede, and the peasants fail to fulfill the task.

When the devil repeats his offer, only Christine, a new arrival in the village, is courageous enough to negotiate with him. She tells him that no Christian would ever give away an unchristened child, but the devil still insists on this reward. When Christine agrees and the devil kisses her on the cheek to seal their contract, she petrifies for a brief moment. In their despair, the villagers begin to calculate: "What is one unchristened child compared to the suffering of an entire village? The more so as Christine is convinced that she can outsmart the devil." They finally agree to the deal and rejoice once the devil has fulfilled the task demanded by the knight. However, the priest baptizes the next newborn, refusing to hand over a soul. The villagers are happy, united in the belief that they have betrayed the devil. When another woman is about to give birth, Christine feels a burning pain on her cheek: right where the devil kissed her, a black spot starts to emerge and turns into a black spider. Many more tiny spiders hatch from the spot after the priest manages to baptize this second child. No one wants anything more to do with Christine because of her distorted face.

From then on, people and cattle start dying of the plague and the villagers agree that this is the devil's way of reminding them of their contractual obligations. Christine finally convinces the villagers to hand over the next unbaptized child in order to prevent further harm. Yet, the priest remains steadfast and again baptizes the next child, upon which the devil flees and Christine turns into a spider. As she has touched both the priest and the child, these are doomed to die. Now the villagers start to quarrel amongst themselves, each putting the blame on the others and claiming to have reminded and warned them. Everyone agrees that those who are guilty should be punished, but no one wants to be seen as guilty and punished themselves. Henceforth, nobody is safe from the spider and even the slightest contact leads to death. Any attempt to escape or to kill the spider is futile. Finally, the mother whose child was saved by baptism thanks to the courageous action of the priest, comes up with an idea: she grabs the spider, stuffs it into a hole in one of the wooden window posts and plugs the hole with a cone that has been blessed. Having touched the spider, she, too, is doomed to die. But her deed leads to the vanquishing of the Black Death, i.e. the plague. Peace and quiet return to the valley.

After the grandfather has finished the story, the guests reluctantly return to the table, as they now fear sitting near the black wooden window post. The grandfather is the only one who musters the courage to sit right in front of it. He is convinced that the spider will remain inside it as long as God is not forgotten. As all the guests' thoughts are now occupied with the spider, the grandfather relates the end of the story: Over the following centuries, the villagers remain god-fearing, everything thrives and they become wealthy. But in keeping with the saying "When God's blessings come in abundance, worms start to appear", the inhabitants of the valley start to fall back into godless behavior over the course of time. In the same way peasants were once mistreated by knights, the former now mistreat their maids and farmhands. For 200 years, the spider remains locked inside the old window post before another female stranger appears in the house. Together with the wife of her son Christen, she torments both people and cattle alike. They also plan to build a new house and leave the old one to the servants. Christen is convinced that the family's happiness depends on the old house, but fails to assert himself in front of the two women.

The servants move into the old house and on Christmas Eve, one of the farmhands removes the cone. Everyone is petrified when the black spider crawls out. Again, almost all the villagers die of the plague and the survivors are outraged, believing that Christen is to blame. All of a sudden, people become religious again, convincing themselves that they have always been so. Only Christen is blamed as being godless. He moves back into the old house and prepares a cone which has been blessed, as his ancestor did, to again lock the spider into its former prison. He is aware that this deed will cost him his life. And indeed, health, peace and wealth return to the village after his death.

200 years later, the old house again becomes uninhabitable. Its owners do not dare to build a new one for quite some time, until a wise man tells them: "You can go ahead and build a new house, but there are two things that have to remain: the old window post with the spider inside, and the old belief that the spider must forever be locked up in its wooden prison. In this way, the new house will also be blessed." (Gotthelf 2002, 115).

When it was time for the grandfather to build a new house, he heeded this advice. The black window post was given its appropriate place, so that neither it nor the events would ever be forgotten. With these words, the grandfather concluded the story and the christening party continued in a cheerful atmosphere. One of his relatives remarked: "It is a pity that we never know how much truth there is in these stories." (Gotthelf 2002, 116).

Many people would nowadays place emphasis on the last sentence, but honestly: Who in this day and age still believes that the devil will lay claim to an unbaptized child? Not many. Irrespective of this belief, the novella touches upon some archetypal topics still of relevance today.

Concepts of Illness Depend on the Zeitgeist

What claims does the novella *The Black Spider* make when it comes to the origins of illness? It was common belief that epidemics – the two historically proven European pest epidemics in the 13th and 15th century – had a metaphysical cause. They were seen as the result of godlessness and a pact with the devil. Natural catastrophes were not simply considered as meaningless fate, but a metaphysical punishment to remind us of the merits of leading a pious life. A god-fearing ego would thus be able to influence natural forces. Beliefs such as these would be doubted by many in today's world with its reliance on vaccines and antibiotics in the face of a contagious disease.

Yet, the novella illustrates fundamentally different views with respect to the devil over the three epochs. Initially, he appears in human form as a huntsman dressed in green and negotiates with Christine. He then metamorphoses into a spider which is locked up, rendering any further dialogue impossible. Christen's mother and wife are not troubled by the spider, they no longer take the devil seriously. Analytical Psychology would argue that religio – the careful consideration of numinous transpersonal forces – is lacking. The two women are simply somewhat negligent and do not actively join forces with the devil like Christine once did. But exactly this negligence is enough to allow the plague to resurface. In the last epoch, during the grandfather's lifetime, the devil only appears in stories. Hence, the perceptual distance to the devil increases with time.

The beginning of this increasing distance and alienation from God and the devil can be traced back to around 1500 AD (Wils 2013, 37ff). Before this date, the world was viewed as an enchanted place, inhabited by tangibly proximate divine and diabolically-devilish creatures, with God as a perceptible presence to be experienced at close hand through divine intervention and purpose. When this belief started to diminish about 500 years ago, a collective process of disembedding set in that resulted in God becoming evermore abstract and inaccessible to people. From then on, his immediate presence became obscure. The same held true for the devil who could no longer be experienced in a tangible manner. Understandably, this raised strong doubts about his and God's existence. Intellectual history knows of another example of this disembedding process. In 1755, Lisbon – one of the wealthiest cities worldwide – was destroyed by an earthquake. On Sunday morning, 1 November, the earth in Lisbon shook for a full ten minutes, followed by fires and floods. At least fifteen thousand people were killed, and numerous buildings and valuable cultural property were destroyed by a combination of the four elements – earth, water, wind and fire.

Did God have a hand in this natural disaster? (Neiman 2004, 18ff, 240ff) Could it be that the Portuguese had burdened themselves with too many sins and punishment was required? An earthquake as a divine cue would tie in with common belief in *The Black Spider*, where villagers were punished with the plague for leading a godless life. On that note, theologians spoke out after the earthquake, claiming that since humans came from dust, would the earth not rise up against the weight of their misdeeds? Yet, the theological idea of punishing sinful humans came with a huge catch: While devout worshippers died beneath the rubble of the church, one single area remained spared by the earthquake, namely Lisbon's red-light district, meaning that only prostitutes, pimps and johns survived. Faith in God's hand protecting honest commoners was severely shaken, and deep cracks appeared in the Church's dictate of fear after the salvation of the "sinners". God did not seem predictable.

In three essays on the Lisbon earthquake (Neiman 2004, 244f), Immanuel Kant adhered to scientific findings on plate theory and – in the spirit of the Enlightenment – classified earthquakes as natural phenomena. One of the insights gained from the quake was that the world was not set up to our advantage. Earthquakes, natural catastrophes or epidemics transcend moral categories and have nothing to do with human failure or godlessness, as these phenomena can be explained on a geological, biological or medical level. The Age of Enlightenment with its orientation towards reason, rationality and natural sciences proved to be an important step towards banishing the image of the enchanted world. And as the novella claims, we do not know how much truth there is in these old tales. We neither want to nor can we believe in divine creation any longer. In the face of natural laws, godliness becomes irrelevant. Faith and prayers seem to be redundant, meaningless, perhaps even dangerous. Taking up this notion in a consistent manner, the title of the first issue of GEO magazine in 2015 reads: "Do we need God?"

From a psychological standpoint, then, we may question whether the self is of any use, or whether it would not be best to renounce it as it hardly has a role to play anymore now that natural phenomena can be explained. This question suggests that the self is an object which we can put aside, and this leads to a further question, namely whether the self exists at all. Is it simply an illusion, as some people claim?

We cannot quite succeed in rejecting the self and its influence on fate altogether: Few people who contract a serious disease or are involved in an accident through no fault of their own would accept this as mere coincidence. The majority would more likely ask why fate has struck in this merciless manner. The loss of a job, a loved one or a fortune is likewise questioned for the sake of obtaining an explanation that transcends the ego and offers new orientation in life.

It would appear that people question fate in dire situations. If things go well, there is a tendency to appropriate the good in an ego-like manner. We tend to forget how many lucky circumstances and external factors beyond our influence have contributed to and had an effect on a positive experience.

Critics may ask whether the terrible events that befall us and we cannot deal with might not trigger a regressive movement towards traditional concepts of the self, since we now find being autonomous and responsible difficult to bear, and we search for a higher power to find purpose in our suffering. We find detachment from the self or its complete loss more difficult in the grimmest hours of existence than when things are going well. One reason for this could be that in parallel to technological advancements, the ego has become not only more autonomous. As Roger Willemsen points out, it has become everything at the same time: more sovereign and more unconscious, more secure yet more instable, more goal-oriented yet more absent-minded (Willemsen 2016, 44).

Contemplating the question of fate in therapy, it seems worth becoming aware of both the therapist's and the patient's more or less unconscious concepts of fate, as they have a tremendous impact on the quest for answers and the therapeutic process. Irritations in the therapeutic relationship, difficulties in transference and counter-transference may occur when differences arise in the interpretation of the appropriate concept of fate, and the resulting unbridgeable gap cannot be respected or tolerated.

The Human Share of Evil

Looking in more detail at the outbreaks of both plagues in the novella, it becomes obvious that similar situations existed before the devil appeared on the scene: humans tortured other humans, disrespected their needs and exploited them. This not only led to pain and suffering, but paved the way for the devil. Analytical Psychology refers to this as the archetypal evil, which in turn is part of the self:

Yet, although the attributes of Christ [...] undoubtedly mark him out as an embodiment of the self, looked at from the psychological angle he corresponds to only one half of the archetype. The other half appears in the Antichrist. The latter is just as much a manifestation of the self, except that he consists of its dark aspect. [...] This great symbol tells us that the progressive development and differentiation of consciousness leads to an ever more menacing awareness of the conflict and involves nothing less than a crucifixion of the ego, its agonizing suspension between irreconcilable opposites. (Jung 1959, CW 9/2, §79)

The Christian image of God includes God and the devil, who is presented as God's son in the Old Testament. Evil and good would thus not be attributed exclusively to the ego-complex and would not be solely individual, but of archetypal quality. From an anthropocentric point of view, there is something evil in the Creation that surpasses human qualities. Hannah Arendt (Arendt 2003, 95) describes this archetypal evil as rootless, and therefore boundless, which might result in evil assuming grave proportions and spreading all over the world. As a transpersonal force, it can seize humans and make them commit terrible deeds.

There are recurring epochs during which knowledge of these evil forces seems to sink into oblivion, as the novella illustrates. New generations forget about the destructive effects that evil can bring. The compulsive repetition coined by Sigmund Freud, then, would not only be described as an individual phenomenon, but also a collective one. We are currently witnessing racism, intolerance and hate which have once again become socially acceptable, despite the horrific events of the 20th century. Attitudes and behaviors that many thought to be overcome are re-surfacing, and neither reason nor facts seem to be sufficiently potent antidotes. The question arises whether society or even humankind as a whole is shying away from venturing into the next step of human evolution, and whether we are in the midst of a collective regression.

The novella suggests a cause for these repetitive phenomena: "When God's blessings come in abundance, worms start to appear." Prosperity harbors the danger of moral, intellectual and ethical neglect. Decadence could therefore be an archetypal shadow aspect of prosperity. As early as 1725, Giambattista Vico described this process as follows: "Men first feel necessity, then look for what is useful, next attend to comfort, still later amuse themselves with pleasure, then grow dissolute in luxury, and finally go mad and waste their inheritance." (cited from Willemsen 2016, 44 *).

Psychologically speaking, this decadence is a lack of self-relatedness, perhaps because people no longer believe in their own influence or have fundamental doubts about their existence. Such lack of self-relatedness facilitates barbaric behavior, which may be understood as a form of regression to an animal stage of development.

The Burden of Guilt

The novella recounts that no one wants to accept responsibility after the first outbreak of the plague. Everyone blames somebody else and wants to see others punished. After the second outbreak of the plague, the villagers convince themselves that they have always lived a pious life instead of being decadent.

Dealing with human guilt in this way is highly topical: We tend to find scapegoats because we are engaged in an ongoing struggle to face our personal share of guilt or failure.

Just think of the bandwagon effect, when repressive regimes collapse, their supporters refute any personal involvement and tone down their own responsibility. They purport that the majority of the people went along with things, implying that destructiveness can be seen as a practical habit that can be donned or removed like a coat, as suits the situation. Yet adopting responsibility for one's own wickedness on a mental, social and perhaps even penal level is extremely difficult to do. Not being tagged as a good or entirely honorable person is a difficult thought to bear. In psychological terms, we need to learn to accept our own shadow, our part of the immoral and unethical. Jung considers the self as an authority of ethical conscience, in which guilt and innocence, as well as feelings of guilt are rooted:

> So long as the self is unconscious, it corresponds to Freud's superego and is a source of perpetual moral conflict. If, however, it is withdrawn from projection and is no longer identical with public opinion, then one is truly one's own yea and nay. The self then functions as a union of opposites and thus constitutes the most immediate experience of the Divine which it is psychologically possible to imagine. (Jung 1958, CW 11, §396)

The self would thus be closely interlinked with a collective moral concept, and as soon as this changes, the image of God changes accordingly and vice versa.

If collective morality no longer remains effective, bitterness can arise as a result of a crumbling interpretation of the world. An example would be a deeply religious woman who abruptly turned away from her faith when she was diagnosed with cancer at the age of 80. She felt she did not deserve this illness at the end of a decently led life, and being no longer able to deal with such a destructive God, she became deeply embittered.

Marie-Louise von Franz (von Franz 1990, 136) defines such bitterness as a disruptive relationship between the ego and the self. Anger or other emotions cause a person to turn inwards and become hardened.

What is important in this context is the difference between a collective, traditional morality and a personal interpretation of what is right and wrong. Any gap between collective and personal assessments calls upon individuals to show their true colors: Do I agree or disagree with the group's set of values? The novella revolves around this conflict, and it is only here that guilt is affirmed:

The young Christen is burdened with guilt because he differed from what God wanted him to be – and he is aware of this. The fact that he bowed to the will of his mother and wife is regarded as his fault. In the language of Analytical Psychology, we could say that he did not consider what his self exacted, instead submitting to the will of others. Hence, the question is how the ego solves the conflict between the different moral authorities in the self, and whether it sacrifices individual certainty in order to avoid perhaps exhausting confrontations with collective values. Some depth psychologists would speak of a false self in this respect, but in my opinion, the self-concept of Analytical Psychology does not recognize a false self. I would therefore say that the ego displaces a belief that is anchored in the self, either to avoid trouble or because it seems unreasonable, unconventional or outdated.

Hannah Arendt (Arendt 2003) reminds us that in Latin, Greek and French, among others, conscience and consciousness were originally synonymous, which is why the request of the Oracle of Delphi to "know thyself", intends us to also always examine our conscience. Ethics is therefore based on an inner dialogue between humans and themselves, with their self. In conversing with the self, right and wrong become distinguishable, and moral questions are clarified. Two things need to be considered here: An ethical attitude is only ethical if I do not allow exceptions in my favor. If we, for example, appropriate something illegally, but in turn condemn those who steal it from us, we have no moral stance. Furthermore, we should not put ourselves in a situation where we despise ourselves, because we would then have to live and continuously wake up and go to bed with this self-contempt.

The Devil in Today's World

It would not be possible to sacrifice an unbaptized soul, an innocent child, in today's world in exchange for the health of an entire village. However, the concept is not so outdated, because even today in certain situations, the question arises whether innocent persons can be sacrificed for the common good. On 17 October 2016, after watching the film "Terrorism – Your Verdict" on German national television, 600 000 viewers were asked to vote on whether a fighter pilot should be allowed to shoot down a hijacked plane with 164 passengers on board in order to prevent a terrorist from deliberately flying it into a stadium filled with 70 000 people. Should someone be allowed to commit murder to prevent an even worse incident? In Germany, Austria and Switzerland, democratic states where homicide is punishable by law, more than 80 percent of those asked said they would argue in favor of the pilot's acquittal.

The (symbolic) devil certainly plays a role in this context, as demonstrated in the statement made by leading US politicians following the terrorist attack on the World Trade Center on 11 September 2001. The suicide bombers were described as devils in the flesh who had to be annihilated. If Gotthelf's novella is considered to contain archetypal knowledge, it is that the devil cannot be eradicated. Instead, ethical diligence on the part of all individuals is required to confront the darker aspects of their personality. But as mentioned previously, it is difficult to look one's own wickedness, one's own shadow, in the eye.

Projection is a commonly used avoidance strategy to seek relief, preferably directed at women and foreigners to this day. This is also reported in the novella: It is not the local farmers who dare to sup with the devil, but Christine, who has recently moved to the village. The feminine in league with the devil as reflected by Eve in Paradise, in Gnostic texts of the second century A.D., in medieval witch burnings or the abortion of female fetuses on the grounds that boys are more valuable than girls is a common motif. Incidentally, the so-called Islamic State is also convinced of the devilish potency of women, because a fighter killed at the hand of a woman cannot allegedly enter paradise. Such notions also affect our society, for example when men lay the blame for their sexual assaults on women whose seductive skills they feel at the mercy of.

The novella has not lost its topicality as far as being foreign is concerned, as that which is evil, threatening or bad is again projected onto strangers, refugees or outcasts. This, too, could be indicative of collective regression, because turf wars and territorial demarcations are behavioral patterns which we share with our animal relatives. Perhaps these collective struggles for demarcation between peoples are unconscious compensatory counter-movements to globalization. In his book *On Aggression*, Konrad Lorenz (Lorenz 1968, 238f) explained some 50 years ago that rats defend their territory against foreign conspecifics and usually kill intruders. Lorenz therefore gave a tribe of rats the opportunity to sniff at a rat from another tribe for one day. When it was put into the cage of the enemy rat tribe a short time later, it no longer ended up being killed. At least among rats, aggressive tendencies were significantly reduced after rats from different tribes were given the opportunity to sniff at and slowly get to know each other.

Spiders and Stones as Symbols of the Self

Spiders and stones were recurring motifs in the dreams of a woman who complained about her fears at the beginning of therapy. After several months, her symptoms increasingly worsened and within a few days, she was no longer able to eat or drink, but just became frozen in silence. A life-threatening stupor had set in. A few days before the onset of these severe depressive symptoms, the patient had dreamt of a spider. Helpless and petrified, she had watched a black spider run away in her dream and felt a leaden heaviness upon waking. Shortly before the stupor set in, the patient again dreamt that she was being stoned to death in the marketplace after moving her bed there. Spiders and stoning are both common dream motifs. Stoning someone to death is a method of execution which has been practiced for centuries. Even nowadays, women are punished in this way in certain countries for committing adultery. Both spiders and stones are considered as symbols of the self:

> [...] the self [...] Theriomorphic symbols are the dragon, snake, elephant, lion, bear, and other powerful animals, or again the spider, crab, butterfly, beetle, worm, etc. (Jung 1959, CW 9/1, §315)

and

If, however, you review the numerous symbols of the self, you will discover not a few among them that have no characteristics of human personality at all. [...] geometrical configurations like the sphere, circle, square, and octagon, or chemical symbols like the Philosophers' Stone, the ruby, diamond, quicksilver, gold, water, fire, and spirit [...] (Jung 1958, CW 11, §276)

The patient experienced devastating aspects of the self and would not have come out of her stupor without inpatient and drug treatment. A few months after her symptoms had gone into remission, the patient was able to explain that she had felt physically petrified during her stupor and at the same time, exposed to an inner storm of intense aggression. She had had a feeling of having lost all boundaries. Even an old guilt had resurfaced which had not been atoned for in the past. Although it was clearly not personal, strangely enough, she was still under the impression that it was her duty to bring it up. Against the background of this description, her stupor might be understood as a compensatory reaction of the unconscious in order to prevent a fragmentation of the ego-complex caused by an uncontrollable outburst of aggression.

Nonetheless, this numb stupor was life-threatening and could not be controlled by the ego-complex. The ego had lost all freedom. As a result of these experiences and dreams, the patient spent many months after remission delving into her family history and stumbled across old family secrets. Although she was not accountable for events which had occurred before her time, she felt responsible for dealing with them. It seemed important to her to learn about the past, as it was similarly important to the grandfather in the *Black Spider*. Historical events must never be forgotten, because they are of transgenerational significance for the present. If the advice in the novella is "not to forget the purport with which the spider was trapped", then a mindset is called for that is aware of the attitude needed to face destructive forces. It is all about *religio*, the careful consideration of the self, not least to prevent the ego from becoming reckless or arrogant. The ego is not responsible for the devil or God, but for its behavior towards them.

A year later, the patient again dreamt of a stone: she was given a gemstone which was placed on her navel. Now the stone's completely different quality, that of value, emerged in contrast. This individual dream image is reminiscent of ancient religious symbols: In Jewish tradition, the Holy of Holies in the Temple of Jerusalem is a stone, the "eben schetijah". It was the "navel" of the world from which all development emanated. At the same time, it was the place where people could connect with God. The black stone of the Kaaba also has religious connotations for Islam: it symbolizes the Holy of Holies in the inner courtyard of the sacred mosque in Mecca and must be circumambulated seven times by pilgrims. According to tradition, this stone is said to have come from paradise. And in Christianity, Christ was the stone that the builders rejected, and Peter was the rock on which the church was to be built. Finally, Jacob sat on a stone, dreaming of a ladder that stretched from heaven to earth. In applying these archetypal images to the world of dreams, Analytical Psychology holds that this denotes the relationship between the ego (dreamer) and the self (stone on the navel), from which new life can be born. It not only represents something that is eternally and indestructibly at work behind finite life, but also the value that can be attributed to horrifying experiences.

Machsal[4]

The philosopher Odo Marquard is said to have coined the term *Machsal* to describe the repression of what was once uncontrollable. *Machsal* reduces the fateful and expands the human sphere of influence and power, thus correlating with growing ego competence and ego autonomy. *Machsal* changes the way in which we deal with illness, birth or death. Dramatic changes have taken place in this sphere in recent decades, altering our image of humans and God. In the fight against death, for example, the question arises as to whether we should use technical know-how to produce test-tube children as a survival aid for the sick, as featured in the US-American film drama *My Sister's Keeper*: A married couple is confronted with a life-saving decision when their young daughter Kate is diagnosed with leukemia. They decide to conceive another genetically perfect daughter as a suitable organ donor for the child suffering from cancer, as neither they nor their son are a suitable match. Their test-tube daughter Anna is a savior sibling with a specific purpose: she becomes a life-sustaining reservoir of spare parts for her terminally ill older sister, whose life depends entirely on her. Stem cells and bone marrow are repeatedly extracted from Anna, and the two sisters have to undergo lengthy hospital stays. The mother gives up her law practice to care for her sick child, channeling all her energies into the survival of her daughter. When her older sister's kidneys finally fail, Anna remains the only possible donor, but now 13 years old, she takes a momentous decision: although she has a very close relationship with her sister, she refuses to donate a kidney, claiming that from now on, she wants control of her own body. As a minor, she sues her parents with

4. Translator's note: *Machsal* is a constructed word and a wordplay on the German word *Schicksal* (=fate), alluding to the fact that humans can influence their fate. It has no direct English equivalent.

the help of a lawyer to obtain the right of self-determination over her body.

The film depicts the possible consequences of subjecting formerly fateful impositions to the influence of the ego. In former times, we could hurl our anger, our feelings of powerlessness, but also our hope at God, because he allowed us to die too early, miserably, without reason, or hoping for a miracle, but nowadays, we have to deal with all this by ourselves in many spheres of life. Psychologically speaking, self-realization becomes ego-realization, self-confidence becomes ego-confidence, and self-optimization is actually ego-optimization. As a consequence, a once metaphysically located, non-human guilt has become humanized and imposed on the ego-complex. The film uses Kate's mother to exemplify what this challenge means: she experiences her obsession with the idea of defying the death of her leukemia-stricken daughter. In doing so, she loses her freedom, meaning her ego is trapped in an autonomous complex that could be referred to as a God complex. All those around her recognize this, except she herself. Stuck in the middle of this complex, her actions become increasingly brutal and ruthless, with the result that she alienates herself from her husband and her children.

3. Borderline Experiences: Birth and Death

From Home to Hospital – Childbirth as a Medical Procedure

Birth and death have been embedded in religious concepts and rituals since time immemorial, and Christianity has placed its trust in baptism and the last rites for the past 2000 years. In existential borderline situations, when we come into contact with the infinite, the incomprehensible, or the uncanny – we refer to the self. It is impossible to imagine these transitional experiences without medical support in today's world. The related opportunities and risks, hopes and fears are becoming an increasingly frequent topic in psychotherapy.

Quite an outrage was caused recently when an employer told a pregnant staff member that pregnancy is not an illness. He actually wanted to attune her to the idea that placing a basic trust in the natural course of events was a reasonable expectation. The pregnant woman found his attitude unacceptable; she felt it was important to take care of herself as a preventive measure at the earliest stage possible so as to not endanger the child she was expecting, and working was hence no longer an option for her. This is not an exceptional case: more and more women are withdrawing from professional life at the earliest stage possible even though neither they nor their unborn children are actually sick.

Basically, pregnancy and childbirth have usually gone well without medical support since time immemorial, but nowadays, medicine in the Western world has almost exclusively taken over responsibility. It has become normal for most women to give birth in a hospital. At the beginning of the 1960s, this was a completely new experience for many women in rural areas of southern Germany, including a currently 85-year-old whom I will refer to as Ms. Miller. She told me about the birth of her youngest child in 1962, for which she was hospitalized for the first time in her life – not because a complication was expected, but because it had become common practice. At the hospital, she was overwhelmed by a deep sense of shame in front of the doctor as she had never been to a gynecologist before. The doctor's presence during birth also compromised her self-esteem and she began to doubt whether she would have been able to give birth without his support. For many months, she feared that she would not be able to love her hospital-born child as much as she loved her other children, which made her feel guilty. Aggravating the situation was the fact that as a young woman, she was reluctant to share her inner conflict with someone; it took decades before she was able to communicate these feelings as a patient during psychotherapy.

Her emotions surfaced at the intersection between existing traditions and newly established conventions. Although such feelings cannot be generalized, they do shed light on some aspects of collective transformation processes. Against the background of what has become acceptable in modern medicine, feelings of shame in patients are not entirely surprising, because nowadays, medicine allows for procedures to be conducted that were once forbidden in other eras or cultures.

Doctors are now permitted to examine all orifices and touch body parts which used to be strictly taboo. Without such invasive procedures, modern medicine could not be practiced successfully. However, since taboos are nowadays suspected of being nothing more than the legacy of old-fashioned people, some patients tend to play down or suppress their feelings of shame because they do not want to be considered either unfashionable or ungrateful. However, if unpleasant feelings are suppressed or repressed on a rational level, they might in turn become a stress factor and complicate treatment.

Giving birth to a child in hospital has become a widely accepted standard. Normality creates a feeling of security in many people, in line with the conviction that if many people are doing it, it must be alright, reasonable and appropriate. Medical support is certainly helpful when it comes to high-risk pregnancies and cases of illness in either mother or child. After all, maternal and infant mortality rates in industrialized countries have decreased dramatically since the beginning of the 20th century due to improved medical care.

Before medical progress was made, women and their mid-wives had to rely on their own knowledge, nature and God for hundreds of thousands of years. Thanks to the achievements of modern medicine, we have moved on and no longer need to trust in fate, nature or God, but mainly in knowledge. This paradigm shift may be illustrated by the following example: Malayans in New Guinea (Vonessen 1998, 34) would try to ease a pregnant woman's labor by opening all the doors, windows and cupboards in the house that were normally kept locked. We have replaced the belief in such analogies with the faith in biological and medical phenomena. The conjurer of this analogy could merely hope to open all the doors possible – quite literally so when chanting the birth spell – to encourage success. Yet, the event had to set itself in motion and an auspicious arrival could only be hoped for. In this respect, modern medicine has facilitated the transformation of humans from hopeful to willing beings.

What changes in attitude might have accompanied the transfer of childbirth from the home to a hospital environment? Over long periods of history, women were at the mercy of the childbirth process. The first birth especially was and still is a completely new and unknown experience for any woman, during which she becomes one of Mother Nature's tools. She is at the mercy of contractions that start spontaneously and at an unknown point in time. By submitting to the rhythm of natural events, by "going along", she can give birth to the child – but never without risk or danger. In cases of uncomplicated spontaneous births, the mother experiences pain and helplessness on the one hand, yet she is actively involved in the birth process and, after giving birth, can enjoy happiness, pride and a sense of self-esteem on the other. In mastering the situation, the female ego withstands an archetypal event.

In hospital, a woman in childbirth is supported by doctors and medical technology and not left on her own. Decisions are made on her behalf. While this brings a lot of advantages, the woman at the same time loses part of her former independence and may therefore feel weaker and less competent. This is perhaps the reason why in Germany more women with uncomplicated pregnancies are reverting to homebirths and a familiar environment where they feel more confident and independent than in the clinic.

Contrary to the increasing desire for home births, more and more women are opting for a birth by scalpel. In Germany and Switzerland, for example, slightly more than 30% of all births are currently carried out by caesarean section, ten times more than 70 years ago and twice as many as 20 years ago. In some major Brazilian cities, the caesarean section rate has risen to 90%. Young doctors and midwives in hospitals there rarely ever experience a natural birth, as medical intervention has become the norm and spontaneous births an exotic exception. As a result, much knowledge about the natural birthing process has been lost, and some doctors no longer want to assist in a spontaneous birth.

Once caesarean sections become a normality, a new and emotionally relieving sense of security is created, meaning that opting for a spontaneous birth has become a burden and now needs to be justified. When someone opposes common standards, they feel the pressure of having to justify themselves. This is exactly what women who want to give birth at home are confronted with today. Their unconventional behavior entails taking on more responsibility themselves than they had previously when home births were absolutely normal.

The WHO currently estimates that only 15% of all births would require a caesarean section, which means that statistically, every second caesarean intervention is not performed on urgent medical grounds. Fear of giving birth has certainly always existed, and it would not be surprising if this fear were on the rise today, because paradoxically, fear tends to increase in times where we enjoy greater security, feasibility and predictability. The prospect of being able to avoid labor pain and fear by opting for a caesarean section is enticing, the more so since no woman knows how "strong" she will be, how much she will be able to endure and whether she can rely on her inner resources before the birth itself. Whereas a spontaneous birth begins at an unknown point in time and in an unknown way, and is unpredictable in terms of duration and progression, a caesarean section is a modern trend fully integrated in today's normal workflow: it takes little time and the course of events is predictable to a large extent.

It is economically reasonable: there is no need to take into consideration over-tired doctors and understaffing in the medical team because of the sudden onset of a birth. Existing medical and technical resources can be optimized, everything can be planned well in advance and controlled by all parties involved.

While women play an active part in natural birth, their role is completely passive during a caesarean section, and there is no moaning and screaming during contractions. The procedure has become a virtually discreet event, no longer inconvenienced by the hefty emotions associated with natural birthing. A caesarean section turns the actual birth into an imperceptible event, as the woman giving birth is cut off from conscious sensual and emotional experience and her role during the process becomes practically meaningless. Initiation into motherhood during this borderline experience is expunged. Perhaps some women have a "bad" feeling after a caesarean section and consider themselves as not fully adequate, because they were spared the pain of labor on the one hand, but have at the same time missed out on an essential human experience on the other.

Bad feelings or even resentment, however, also exist among women on whom a caesarean section is performed because the natural birth they wanted was not possible. A young mother who once found herself in this situation remarked, "This is no child of mine." The fact that the birth of her child did not go according to plan was experienced as a narcissistic injury. Mothers such as her feel no gratitude for the medical contribution to their health and that of their child, and it becomes clear that the desire for a natural birth can also be viewed as "a matter of principle".

Reproductive Medicine

Medicine has become a response to demands. By this I mean that for quite some time now, doctors have not been solely treating illnesses, but have increasingly catered to their patients' wishes. If you present the German state health insurance scheme with the diagnosis "desire to have children met", they are likely to pay for a tubal ligation. Couples who remain involuntarily childless despite an intense desire to have children are entitled to be diagnosed as having "a desire to have children", since the most advanced medical technology stands ready to help them get pregnant. The state health insurance will cover part of the reproductive medical costs, i.e. fertility treatment. Society has thus accepted an unfulfilled desire for children as a medical diagnosis.

One of the first decisions that couples who opt for fertility treatments have to take is to disclose their intimate sexual habits to a doctor. If in vitro fertilization is an option, the woman's body is subjected to a number of demanding procedures, from hormone therapy to anesthesia during egg collection. The man's physical integrity and intimacy is much more protected during sperm donation. He can masturbate freely in a cabin without being disturbed or observed.[5] Theologian Stephan Wehowsky (Wehowsky 1988, 53) emphasizes that in the course of in vitro fertilization, a new relationship is created, including a legitimate triangular one. The doctor – who is usually a man – succeeds in something that the partner has so far failed to achieve, namely helping the woman to have a child. As a powerful helper, he seems to be more potent than

---

5. Some European countries now allow not only sperm, but also egg donations. Although donating an egg is physically much more demanding than donating sperm, unlike sperm donors, women are not financially compensated, i.e. they must in fact donate their own eggs. This inequality is not plausible, but positively discriminatory.

her partner, and could therefore play a role in her imagination, with the result that any one of the three persons involved can be overwhelmed by strong emotions.[6]

During in vitro fertilization, the woman becomes the egg supplier and the man the sperm donor. Sexuality and procreation are separated: sexual intercourse is now only *one* method of reproduction.

We learn that footballer Cristiano Ronaldo has had three and entrepreneur Nicolas Berggruen two children delivered by a surrogate mother. This approach ensures that the children "belong" to them and they do not have to have anything more to do with the birth mother after the delivery. Thanks to modern medicine, men have become independent of mothers who could claim sole custody or sue them for high maintenance payments. By opting for surrogacy, these wealthy men have spared themselves such legal disputes.

It seems that in the not too distant future, wealthy people will be able to renounce the respective other sex entirely if they want to have children. Research into the production of our own eggs and sperm is quite advanced. Genetically speaking, it will become possible to father a child with oneself and have a one-parent baby. Will this technology, then, turn the religious concept of a virgin pregnancy into earthly reality, as we accept it in the Bible in Mary?

And is industry about to convince us that the best thing to do is not to risk natural reproduction in the first place? In view of the very slight chance of producing defective eggs or sperm, might we be persuaded to rely on a safe and planned

---

6. A sperm donor can experience himself as an object that needs to deliver. Feelings of irritation can arise, which are often suppressed. Similarly, measures taken before in vitro fertilization can put an extreme strain on a partnership, for example if sexuality has to be organized in line with the ovulation calendar. When sexuality is organized for the prime purpose of fertilization, it can turn into an ordeal.

procedure, allegedly knowing what we are going to get right from the start? Biochemist Erwin Chargaff (Wehowsky 1988, 58) suspects that human reproduction could increasingly move away from the sexual domain to a semi-industrial production, thus becoming mechanized and commercialized. In this way, human and animal procreation is becoming much more akin than many people realize, as artificial insemination in some animals, such as horses and cows, is already a routine procedure carried out by veterinarians. Medicine has raised the reproduction of humans and animals to the same level.

Through the application of in vitro fertilization, the child has become less of a gift and is rather the result of a laboratory team's efforts. It is manufactured with a certain, and with all probability increasing, degree of reliability. As with other products, the emphasis is on quality, and customers' demands will increase in those areas where the possibility exists. Those manufacturers who are able to produce the most beautiful, most intelligent, the most docile or successful offspring will be in great demand, and the human image could become ruthlessly perfect. In view of the culture of increased customer service mentality, we could end up having to issue a certificate of guarantee for the child to be created, and that child will not be accepted unless it is perfect. And if the child produced turns out to be defective, with whom will the responsibility lie, who will be to blame and who will be held liable? And what will happen to faulty children? Can they be rejected and returned?[7]

When it comes to enhancing human beings, then humankind in its present form is no longer acceptable. There is indeed something inhumane about this notion and the blame

---

7. The fairy tale of the Brothers Grimm "Hans my hedgehog" describes how a planned child who does not meet the expectations of its parents at all, still develops his personality and talents and becomes king, i.e. the most important man in the state. (Daniel 2015, 107)

can no longer be attached to God or fate. In case of failure, we direct our anger or grief at those who are at its cause. While God, or rather fate, has always got off scot-free for any "mistakes", humans can be held accountable. That is why we need so many insurance companies to relieve the individual and ultimately pass on compensation payments to the collective whole. The individual would be overwhelmed by the liability. Further improvements will increase related risks and inevitably, insurance premiums. The consequences of this immense personal responsibility are dramatic: In the USA, it seems that fewer and fewer doctors are willing to work in obstetrics, the branch in which most lawsuits for malpractice occur and huge financial compensations are normally at stake.

In my opinion, it would be worthwhile exploring what significance and impact the different places of procreation have on human development: natural human procreation takes place in the warm, dark uterine cavity. During in-vitro fertilization, the developing embryo is temporarily exposed to great physical cold and brightness. What is more, the sperm does not penetrate the egg by itself, but is injected into it with a sharp object. It would be naive to think that these interventions do not have any consequences for human development and identity, because they are stored in the body's unconscious. Yet test-tube children would not be alive if this method did not exist, and this medical achievement which has helped to outsmart Mother Nature can be welcomed. On a mythological level, this progress can be understood as a continuation of promethean acts: In the tradition of Prometheus, who stole fire from the gods to make people less dependent on the whims of nature, we are constantly increasing our know-how and thus, our autonomy from natural laws. Our intention to overcome nature ultimately includes the desire to be able to do without human mothers altogether. In 2016, scientist Ali Brivanlou from Rockefeller University in New York managed to grow an embryo for 12 days in a culture medium which mimicked the uterine wall. In a statement, he remarked: "Surprisingly, our system allowed normal development at least for the first twelve days, despite the complete lack of maternal input." Use of the word *normal* is interesting here – perhaps the intention is to help raise acceptance of further laboratory experiments.

Even if it were proven biologically possible one day to grow a person outside of the womb, the question of how this will affect the individual arises, as the newborn will have had to put up with all these technical interventions. Whether we deal with nature or technology, it is and remains a matter of fate, which will sometimes rather fall outside of and sometimes rather within the sphere of human responsibility, whose different forms will influence our relationships. When we think of the resentment some children already harbor at the name chosen for them by their parents, the question arises as to what will happen when they find out about the technical interventions initiated on their behalf – which, by the way, are often concealed from children. It seems that many people who have made use of these modern technologies still feel uncomfortable about admitting them, at least for the time being, which is why completely new types of family secrets are in the making.

In terms of human identity, new ground was broken in Mexico in 2016, when a child with three biological parents was born – two mothers and a father. The nucleus of an egg from the original mother was transferred to a previously enucleated egg from a donor. The second mother provided only the egg cell envelope and the so-called mitochondrial DNA. The purpose of this treatment was to prevent a hereditary disease in the child.

Do we not dare to encroach upon what was previously divine territory with one-parent or three-parent babies? And are we in awe or do we shudder at this prospect? Still, the urge to cross boundaries is part of human nature, as repeatedly mentioned. Some people are too optimistic about the opportunities, others too pessimistic about the dangers. In the 19th century, for example, people were too pessimistic when they feared serious damage to health would be caused by the speed of train travel. A broad spectrum of emotions ranging from enthusiasm to rejection emerges at the intersection between innovation and tradition. Becoming aware of the underlying longings and fears at best helps us develop an attitude that is neither too critical nor too euphoric.

Artificial insemination combined with prenatal diagnostics and other medical procedures could lead to the subordination of human dignity to healthcare and its optimization. In many areas of medicine, the general promise that we will recover is fulfilled, which often makes us happy and grateful – but the result of this could be that human value and dignity will increasingly be defined by one's health. Dignity, then, would seem not to be a basic entitlement, but subject to the existence of certain more or less inherent qualities or abilities, which in the worst case may no longer be present. This trend is particularly well accepted in societies with a tendency to judge their members based on merit.

For quite some time, death has also raised questions about human dignity, which can no longer be taken as a given in all cases, but is rather dependent on favorable underlying conditions. Hence, this would now seem an appropriate juncture to take a closer look at contemporary circumstances of death.

From Home to Hospital – Death as a Medical Procedure

French historian Philippe Ariès (Ariès, 2013) pointed out that for centuries, perhaps even millennia, humans have had a presentiment that their final hour was near. Some people about to die would retreat, for example to their favorite place, to die alone in peace. Others sought fellowship. In late medieval France, those dying would often say goodbye to their relatives and acquaintances at home. A priest would frequently be called, and the last will and testament would be announced before all those present. Up until the 18th century, a person would still take their last breath in public in a room full of people – including children. It was not until the beginning of the 19th century that Ariès observed an increasing reluctance among people in industrialized societies to admit their own approaching death. From then on, it was no longer the dying, but the doctors who knew how to interpret the signs of imminent death, and the medical profession started to claim competence in this sphere. It is not surprising then that death and dying gradually disappeared from the familiar everyday world of home and moved to the hospital.

Medical treatment today can considerably postpone the onset of death, blurring the lines between life and death and making the transition between the two more complicated. The question arises: when is someone "really" dead? Even if "sudden cardiac death" or "clinical death" has been diagnosed, patients can frequently still be resuscitated. Is someone diagnosed as brain dead really dead, although they still have a rosy complexion, their body is still warm and they look like they are simply lying there asleep? The struggle to find answers to this has been highly controversial and emotional, i.e. complex-laden. As a result, death is no longer determined by physiological parameters alone, but by definition. This may cause discomfort for some individuals, because their senses perceive otherwise and they risk being berated as unreasonable. However, we should not forget that brain death is treated from an outside perspective, and nobody knows anything about this condition from the inside; we are left with assumptions and beliefs, at least to some extent.

If a socially agreeable definition of brain death were to be decided upon, this would have far-reaching consequences, because the organs of a healthy brain-dead person can be "recycled", in other words the body then becomes something of value and use. The Japanese reject this notion, believing that all parts of the human body – and not just the brain – are inhabited by a person's spirit. Therefore, if each part of the body contains a fraction of the spirit, should one organ be transplanted, then that individual's personality is violated (Lafontaine 2010, 68). In cultures where brain death is perfectly acceptable, on the other hand, organ transplants can be seen as a method of reintroducing organs into the cycle of life. The individual organs, not the entire body, experience a resurrection of the flesh, and this is quite definitely medical progress and no longer a Christian myth. Using the organs of a deceased human being has only become possible in the Western world because of a general shift in our attitude towards corpses and death since the Age of Enlightenment. Up until then, people experienced a sense of the supernatural in the presence of a corpse, which was considered as uncanny and treated with either awe or disgust. In the Middle Ages, people still felt threatened by "the Otherworld" and believed it necessary to keep the living dead at a distance from this world by erecting cemetery walls and grates at the entrance, the so-called witch grates, which were supposed to act as leg-breakers, similar to those used for cattle.

Nobody today would consider such protective measures to be necessary, and both demythologization and the lifting of taboos has meant that dead bodies have become a commodity which can be used or not. Now that the organs of brain-dead people are up for sale, this has become more than evident. Quite some of us feel that our corpse might even become an unreasonable burden for our relatives who will ultimately have to bear the cost of gravesite upkeep. In an attempt to cut these costs for our families, we opt for an easy-to-care-for and inexpensive final resting place, thus opening the way for cheaper coffin imports from Eastern Europe or making price comparisons between undertakers common – a practice which would have been considered irreverent in the past.

Who Owns Death?

According to Philippe Ariès, a papal document from the Middle Ages assigned doctors the duty of informing people of their imminent death if they themselves had not noticed that they were dying (Ariès 1976, 160). From about the 19th century onwards, doctors only spoke out when their opinion was expressly sought, and this with reluctance; such practice continued well until the end of the 20th century, when it became common for people to keep the truth about dying from the one nearing death. In this way, a dying person was not only spared, but also deprived of their autonomy and self-determination, because from that point on, doctors and relatives took all the essential decisions on their behalf. This disempowerment – and Ariès even speaks of expropriation – of the dying person was intended for their own good, but made it more difficult for the person in question to prepare for death.

A landmark decision taken by the Federal Court of Justice in Germany in 2010 strengthened the right of self-determination of patients as it allows doctors to terminate life-prolonging measures at a time when the patient is not yet close to death. The presumed will of the patient, even if they are not in a conscious state, is the one that counts. Thanks to legal clarification, death may now resume its natural course, if so desired.

Yet, this regained freedom is not enough for everyone, and some people insist on even greater self-determination, namely the right to request euthanasia – a desire that is reminiscent of the attitude of the Stoics, who regarded suicide as justified in cases of incurable illness or unavoidable poverty. As soon as someone expressed a will to die, the reason was publicly declared before the Senate, and if the Council agreed, the citizen would receive poison from the authorities in order to be able to end their life. At the time, however, suicide was prohibited for soldiers and slaves on the grounds of patriotic and economic reasons.

While neither the Old nor the New Testament condemn suicide (Alvarez 1990, 68f), the Middle Ages were far less tolerant, proscribing that the end of life had to be placed in divine hands. It was one's duty to live and to place the fruits of one's labors into the hands of the monarch. Suicides were thought to be under the devil's spell, their corpses subjected to terrifying exorcist rites and their goods usually confiscated. However, the nobility and clergy were spared from these measures, and should they commit suicide, they were thought of as having an upright moral character. At the beginning of the 17th century, a new way of thinking emerged with the English physician Robert Burton who claimed that the cause of suicide was not satanic obsession, but melancholy. In his opinion, a suicidal person was not to be seen as a criminal or victim of the devil, but had to be treated as a patient. This view fell on fertile ground, and in 1751, the suicide offence act disappeared from the Prussian, and 40 years later from the French Code. In the 19th century, suicide finally came under medical cognizance.

People who decide to commit suicide are usually alone, having broken off relationships with other people; they act secretly and risk failure. Active euthanasia, a form of modern institutionalization of suicide, on the other hand, can almost be viewed as achieving the opposite: suicide can be carried out in the presence of others at a freely chosen time and with minimal risk; it is calculable, painless and swift, and broadly accepted by society. Euthanasia thus not only conforms to our trending habits for making things easier on ourselves, but also shows phenomenological parallels with the caesarean section.

Death as a Narcissistic Injury

"Nothing is more certain than death, nothing more uncertain than its hour": The second half of the saying, attributed to Anselm of Canterbury, is increasingly perceived as a narcissistic injury by evermore people insisting on the right to choose the time of their own death. For many patients suffering from an incurable disease, suicide is the one alternative to passively awaiting the approach of one's final hour. By choosing the time and manner of death, there is at least the chance of regaining some control over it. In contrast to the classic "suicide", close relatives can be informed of the patient's intention and their consent asked for. Perhaps this desire for euthanasia is, in certain cases, an unconscious cry for attention and acceptance in a world of more and more fragile, unstable and interchangeable relationships and less and less metaphysical security.

Proponents of euthanasia often criticize use of the term "killing oneself with intent" and suggest "self-determined death" as more appropriate. The effect and impact of words in this context is immense. Active euthanasia can be paraphrased as a termination of life upon request, a suicide that is supported or assisted, which does not come over as positively as a "self-determined death". One could not imagine launching an advertising campaign for the termination of life upon request, but advertising for self-determination in death is at least conceivable. Who does not want to be considered as pro-active these days? After all, is being pro-active not one of the most important collective values? The power of words once again becomes apparent when someone who has elected to end their life requests that it be phrased as "assistance with dying" rather than speaking of either suicide or intentional death. Again – who does not want to help others? And who would dare to refuse assistance? Those who reject the notion of euthanasia suppress their disquiet, fearing they might be accused of precisely this failure to provide assistance, and therefore be labeled inhumane.

Euphemism as a conceptual cover-up reminds me of the so-called "culling" of animals, which is nothing more than a mass killing, mostly by employing gas. Such euphemisms spare us painful feelings in the face of cruel reality. This seems to be an important trend to me, namely the attempt to suppress the hefty emotions and terrible experience surrounding death and dying. This is considered good and ideal and is the only kind of death that seems to be dignified. Dignity appears to exist solely under good circumstances. A discreet, unconscious death is idealized, and a new myth is born. Something truly essential takes place in the subconscious state of mind. A structural parallel to the idealized caesarean section becomes apparent, as it is also carried out scream-free and when the mother is in an unconscious state.[8]

Proponents and opponents of active euthanasia are engaged in a heated discussion: what to some is a progressive and contemporary right to self-determination is an expression of a time of decadence to others. Let's take a look at the more than 4000-year-old Berlin Hieratic Papyrus 3024 (Jacobsohn 1952, 1-48), which contains the "conversation of a suicidal person with his soul" – his Ba – which might be a fruitful source for this discussion. According to Jacobsohn, contemporaries of the life-weary man probably experienced the horror and dread of the loss of God for the first time in Egyptian history. Religious ceremonies had become worthless, allegedly being replaced by disorientation and frivolity. Accustomed to a collective cult community, Egyptians were suddenly left to their own devices, which must have been unbearable for them, as reflected in the rising suicide rates. Are we not in a comparable situation today, because traditional images of God and religious concepts have become implausible and have lost their effect? Hence the look at the old text. In the depths of despair, the life-weary writer wishes to die. He knows that the meticulous and careful observation of the death ritual is the only means convincing enough to justify his suicide plan, and wants the gods to examine whether he has the right to depart from this life because of his untenable situation. Not tormented by the thought of killing himself, but by the fear of committing a sin, he then makes a discovery which for an

---

8. If in these two most existential threshold experiences, the collective trend favors a lack of awareness, it is hardly surprising that psychotherapy oriented towards depth psychology is met with suspicion. Indeed, those who dare to take the unconscious into account are to a certain extent willing to give up control of the ego and to relate to something greater than the ego.

Egyptian of that time was probably the most terrible thing that could have happened: His own Ba, the innermost core of his soul, which Analytical Psychology refers to as the voice of the self, offers a certain resistance to his plan. In doing so, the Ba by no means tries to prevent him from carrying out his intentions, but on the contrary, expresses a certain contempt for his indecision:

> "Are you not yourself the man to ward off the fear of 'sin' and to 'disregard' it? A moment ago [...] you wanted to depart this life, now you are concerned about 'the good', as a 'lord of treasures' is concerned about his possessions, i.e. you want to preserve the good scrupulously and be as innocent as a babe." (Jacobsohn 1968, 22)

The harshness and directness of the Ba's short answer illustrates that the suicide's pre-occupation with sin is of no concern to the Ba. It is the suicidal person who must deal with the fear of possible misconduct. For the Ba, the man's entire attitude is flawed, as is his concern for what is formally good. The Ba is obviously concerned about something entirely different, which revolves around the following two aspects:

A premature death – says the Ba – will prevent something yet not visible and unknown from being created, something which might have been able to emerge, and should still have emerged, from the individual and the Ba's life. The Ba is not worried about externally visible deeds as yet undone or incomplete, but about an as yet unconscious inner possibility slumbering deep within the individual with the desire to manifest and develop itself. This possibility would be destroyed if he dies prematurely before it has even had a chance to emerge into the conscious world. Hence, it is all about an incomplete, unfinished life. The second aspect that the Ba alludes to is the quality of the relationship between itself and the life-weary person. To illustrate this point of view, it describes a conflict in the relationship between a husband and wife. The Ba relates the story of a man asking for his dinner to be served at an earlier time than usual and his wife, who refuses. It is not yet evening, the right time has not yet arrived. The husband feels that the woman's negative attitude is a violation of his rights, a threat to his male self-assurance, and he backs off grudgingly.

The Ba compares the suicidal man to the man hardened in his heart and emphasizes that it wants appreciation and respect for its completely different and individual nature. This requires the Ba to assert its own position for which it will be held responsible, and to expect the same of the suicidal man. It is this personal responsibility and not obedience, virtue or harmonious agreement that ought to form the basis of their relationship. Psychologically speaking, a suicidal person should by no means remain in a weaker child-like state, striving to do the right thing and judging own deeds against categories such as "obedience" and "disobedience". The lifeweary man now understands how his anxiety and insecurity have triggered the need for acceptance of his suicide plans. This breakthrough is reached when he realizes that he must bear responsibility for his intention. This newly accepted responsibility is in stark contrast to his fear of sin and makes him aware of his motives for suicide. The Ba then goes on to describe their relationship in the following way:

> You belong in any case to me [...] ... You may continue to be consumed in your grief and finally die of it, or you may gradually "cling to" life again and recover from your grief. [...] For the "home" you were looking for – being one with me, joined in human wholeness – this home we shall have in either case. (Jacobsohn 1968, 47)

What could be the quintessence of the text? In responding to the question of suicide, the Ba vehemently opposes the categories of "sin", "punishment", "right" and "wrong". It is not about convincing others, the soul, society or a higher might of the right to suicide and obtaining consent. The Ba by no means wants to be understood as a punitive authority, but rather encourages people to enter into a partnership at eye level. This is in stark contrast to the image which many Christians have internalized of a potentially punishing God the Father. Someone who doggedly and almost militantly insists on their right to die in discussions on euthanasia, should ask themselves whether they are not unconsciously trapped in an image of a punitive God, in other words, in an authority complex.

Guidelines for Active Euthanasia?

If euthanasia is permitted, questions emerge that transcend current conventions and existing boundaries: Who is permitted to make use of euthanasia? For example, how old must a person with an incurable disease be to be allowed to choose this option? The more so because medicine might make enough progress to treat the disease just a few years later.

May an (old) person who no longer wants to be a burden to others request euthanasia? Or a person for whom life has become meaningless? Someone who has grown tired of living? We need to be aware that as soon as such questions have been regulated by law, society will have succeeded in defining what constitutes an unworthy life. Projections are at least partly at play here because the people making assessments of the quality of life and the will to live are usually those who are not suffering from the symptoms or circumstances mentioned above. What appears plausible from the outside can be quite different subjectively. In this respect, John Donne, Anglican preacher and poet of the 17th century, was careful to refrain from naming the exact specific conditions that would warrant suicide:

> I have deliberately abstained from extending this speech to examples and special rules, [...] because their boundaries are dark, rugged, smooth and narrow and error here is fatal. (quoted from Flaßpöhler 2007, 35 *)

Euthanasia is usually performed by administering a cocktail of drugs which make the person fall asleep, become unconscious and die peacefully. But what if someone wants to shoot themselves with a pistol? Can they be denied the right to choose the method to end their life? And what if a person willing to die wants to do so in a conscious state, i.e. unanesthetized, and requests a knife with which to cut their carotid artery? And what if a person requests to be killed by another person, that is, wants to entrust their death into the hands of someone else? Anyone who wants to grapple with this might be inspired by the film *Emma's Happiness.*[9]

In her book *Mein Wille geschehe – Sterben in Zeiten der Freitodhilfe* (*My will be done – Dying in times of assisted suicide*), Svenja Flaßpöhler reports on Paul Zögli, who determined his own end by assisted suicide (Flaßpöhler 2007, 131). He rates his life as having been almost perfect and points out that he

---

9. It tells the story of Emma, who lives alone as a pig farmer on her grand-father's run-down and hopelessly indebted farm. She treats her pigs lovingly until the last day and slaughters them in a kosher way. Max is a car salesman, also alone, and is diagnosed with pancreatic cancer. He doesn't have long to live. Accidentally, he ends up on Emma's farm and they start a relationship. Max sees how Emma slaughters her pigs, and when he is about to die, he wants her to kill him with the same tenderness, which she does.

has enjoyed it to the fullest. The desire to hold the reins even at the end of his life has always been strong. His greatest fear is therefore that another heart attack will prevent his suicide. The crux of the matter lies in the principle of remaining in control until death.

Often, self-determination is driven by the desire to put an end to terrible suffering. Thus, a man with cancer who decided to end his life compared his suffering to that experienced by Jesus on Calvary, where he died on the cross under unspeakable torture. Jung has also made the connection between the unjust suffering of ordinary people and Christ's death on Calvary. The desperate cry of Jesus on the cross: "My God, my God, why hast thou forsaken me?" (Matthew 27, 46) is – according to Jung (Jung 1958, CW 11, §647) – the moment in which the Son of God suffers the injustice that mortals have to endure every day. Terrible and inhumane things happened on the cross. But according to Jung, Jesus' fate is only sealed when he experiences physical and mental torture and loneliness; in today's world, his view may be uncomfortable and sound cynical to many.

Marie-Louise von Franz (von Franz 1984, 43) has also witnessed the tragedy of ageing people who, due to serious illness and physical weakness, become increasingly dependent on others, and sometimes – as she reports – even subject to the tyranny of relatives or carers. Without wanting to excuse such tyranny, she asked herself whether there could be a deeper sense to this helplessness, namely to enable ego-centeredness to transform itself into ego-consciousness. This would mean no longer imposing one's own will or getting one's own way at any price, but submitting to decisions of the self. Such a commitment would allow feelings of entrapment to be transformed into feelings of support in a greater context, and to let a place of confinement become a place of security within the self, in God. As autonomy and control are seen as desirable or even required in today's world, such a commitment is difficult to make for many, as it is often accompanied by a sense of fear.

4. The Eye as a Symbol of the Self

Being Seen

What's the big deal about being seen? Just as we need air to breathe, we like to be perceived, noticed and mirrored. But being seen carries obvious risks, for example, when we think about depressed patients who feel more exposed to the gaze of others than healthy people. With a growing loss of self-esteem, they imagine themselves to be judged and condemned, guilty and/or ashamed of other people's glances (Hell 2000, 56f). Hence, being seen is not always a positive experience. Being able to see confers a power which, like any other power, can principally be abused.

This is exactly what a woman in her mid-30s felt when she was asked by her psychotherapist to talk about her dreams during sessions. She refused, and her resistance puzzled the therapist until he learned that during her childhood, her father had insisted that the door to her nursery room remain open day and night. Based on this experience, the patient knew exactly how video-monitored prisoners in Guantanamo must feel. As a child, the only refuge that was left to her was the world of her imagination. She created rooms in her fantasy in which she felt free and unobserved, and to which her father had no access. It was only when she sought therapeutic help due to burn-out that she came to realize how much she still felt threatened to this day whenever asked to reveal something about her inner world.

A patient of Gustav Bovensiepen expressed the fear that he, as a therapist, had the power to see everything inside of her, then could take it away and destroy it (Bovensiepen 2009, 143). Because the patient experienced the analyst's observing, mirroring gaze as so destructive, she tried to shield herself from his intrusive sight by wrapping herself in a blanket, among other things. Psychologically speaking, a parental complex was projected onto the analyst, giving him a far-reaching visionary power which could be misused in an aggressive way. Such experiences remind us of the ancient symbol of the self that is known all over the world, namely the all-seeing eye of God. Jung writes:

> The eye is also a well-known symbol for God. (Jung 1959, CW 9/1, §594)

and

> The eye is the prototype of the mandala. (Jung 1959, CW 9/1, §592)

Nothing remains hidden from this divine eye: whether joy, good deeds, or human offence and lovelessness. Although fewer and fewer people believe in such an "all-seeing" eye of God looking from the afterworld to the here and now, the phenomenon has not simply disappeared. Among other things, it can unconsciously evoke fears of guilt and failure or shame, especially when people undergoing difficult situations unconsciously regress to beliefs previously thought overcome or, as mentioned above, project this ability onto authority figures.

The all-seeing eye has now largely moved from the divine to the sphere of human technology, to be found in earthly institutions like the NSA or companies that create personality profiles based on people's internet activities and data. Thus, a part of the former self has virtually migrated into the tangible reality of human life. Understandably, this creates a feeling of discomfort because one cannot avoid being observed on the internet, nor can using social media in a responsible manner protect one's personal data from being viewed, evaluated, sold and utilized.

What is the difference, then, between an all-seeing divine eye and the capabilities of modern surveillance technology? The observer god treats all human beings equally, whereas institutional surveillance establishes a hierarchy within humanity. On the one hand, there are those who have access to data and benefit from it, while on the other hand, the vast majority of people know they are being watched and have to come to terms with it whenever they are on the internet or out and about in public.

Seeing as a Means of Power and Autonomy

The Grimm fairy tale *The Sea Hare* tells us about the impor-tance of an all-embracing vision: The protagonist is a king's daughter who can look out of the 12 windows under the bat-tlements of her castle and see in all directions of her kingdom, both above and under the ground.[10] Nothing remains hidden from her, she is omniscient. This is a fine thing, since she

10. The fact that her view is indeed all-encompassing is indicated by the completeness of the number 12: a year is made up of 12 months, a day of 12 hours.

wants to rule alone and be subject to no one. Those who can see everything have a good chance of retaining their power. Interestingly, the king's daughter extends a relationship offer to the men in her kingdom: whoever can conceal themselves without being found shall become her husband. A relationship would therefore only be possible if a man were able to escape her control. 97 men try in vain and are beheaded. As a warning to further applicants, their heads are displayed in front of the castle. In fact, for a long time no one dares to come forward, which amuses the king's daughter and leads her to believe that she will remain free for the rest of her life.

Let us look at this first part of the fairy tale from a psychological perspective: the ruler finds pleasure in freedom and autonomy, and does not perceive freedom as a form of loneliness or abandonment. If we understand the king's daughter as a representative of the zeitgeist, the fairy tale would take us to a time that sees power, autonomy and independence as highly desirable – which is quite appropriate for our era. Access to surveillance data and comprehensive information are important pillars for maintaining power.

If the fairy tale were to end here, the king's daughter would remain single, without ever being able or allowed to love, trust and hope. This would be a barren situation with no prospects for development, because she would not be able to bear children. Psychologically speaking, there would be no new possibilities, no innovation, but only the sheer retention of power through the exercise of complete control.

The fairy tale does not end in stagnation, though, but continues: Three brothers appear at the royal court to try their luck. Merely looking out of the first window suffices for the king's daughter to discover the oldest brother in a lime pit and the middle brother in the castle cellar. Soon, the 98th and 99th stakes are standing in front of the castle with two more heads upon them. In spite of the death of his two brothers, the youngest also comes before the king's daughter and, knowing full-well how difficult the task is, asks for a day of reflection and three attempts. He wants her to kill him only if he fails at the third attempt. The youngest brother is handsome and asks in such a heartfelt manner that his wish is granted, although the king's daughter tells him frankly that he will not succeed. Based on her previous experience, she has no reason to doubt her vision and feels she runs no risk in being generous. Nevertheless, it is astonishing that in allowing the applicant some leeway, she is not quite so strict.

What does the youngest brother do now? He spends the following day in long, but unsuccessful contemplation. As merely thinking does not help, he decides to go hunting. Hunting is mainly carried out by men, and is an activity where two come together, namely the hunter and the hunted. Successful hunters face their victims. On that note, the decapitated men could be described as the prey of the king's daughter, who tracked them down and killed them. By going hunting, the youngest brother now familiarizes himself with the craftmanship of this dangerous woman and her personality; he wants to get to know her. While hunting, he wants to shoot a raven, but the bird asks for mercy and promises to repay him. The youngest brother agrees and also spares a fish and a fox shortly after. He proves that a skilled hunter can track down his prey, but does not necessarily have to kill it. He can pardon and let others live. The latter is something that the king's daughter has not yet achieved, as her superiority always means that her opponents lose their lives.

As agreed, the young man must now hide from the king's daughter to be hunted. Since he has not yet found a safe hiding place, he asks the raven for a suggestion in return for sparing its life. The bird puts the young man into one of its eggs and sits on it. When the king's daughter approaches the first ten windows, looks out and discovers she cannot see him, she becomes frightened. This is plausible, because no one has ever made it this far, and not knowing everything is quite awful for her. Her fear does not last long, though, because her view through the eleventh window brings her success. The king's daughter has the raven shot, the egg broken and the young man brought out. For the first time, as promised, she finds it in her power to pardon a man and says: "For once you are excused, but if you do not do better than this, you are lost." The next day, as a reward for granting its life, the fish swallows the young man and swims to the bottom of the lake. Again, the king's daughter is dismayed when she finds she cannot see him even from the eleventh window, but relieved when the twelfth window finally reveals his hiding place. The fish must die, she keeps her word and explains to the young man: "Twice you are forgiven, but be sure that your head will be set on the hundredth post."

With a heavy heart and facing his very last chance, the youngest brother approaches the fox in the field and asks him for a safe hiding place. The fox, knowing how difficult the task is, goes to a spring, dives down and reappears as a market stall owner trading in animals. The youngster also has to dive into the water and re-emerges transformed into a little sea hare. The transformed fox wanders off to the city to display the little animal. Many citizens come to see it, including the king's daughter, who eventually buys it for a lot of money. Before handing the sea hare over to the king's daughter, the fox says to him: "When the King's daughter goes to the window, creep quickly under the braids of her hair." Now it is again time for the king's daughter to start peering out of her windows. But she cannot spy the young man, not even from the twelfth window. Such a tremendous fear and anger well up inside her that she lashes out, shatters the glass in all the windows and causes the entire castle to tremble. When she feels the sea hare under her braid, she throws it to the ground and shouts: "Away with you, get out of my sight!" Faced with her own powerlessness, she no longer wants any living creature around her, and longs to be alone again, which is when she feels most comfortable. As long as she has control over everything, she feels strong, however, her inner fragility and instability become apparent when she loses power.

The sea hare runs away to the fox, both hurry to the spring, dive in and regain their original appearance. The young man thanks the fox, attesting him with great wisdom. The fairy tale ends with the king's daughter accepting her fate and marrying the young man, who finally becomes king. He never tells her where he hid at the third attempt, which is probably why she assumes that he accomplished this using his own faculties and skill and thus, is more adept than her. She can therefore respect and maybe even fear him a little. As a woman who was highly successful on her own, she does not have the vision to accept that teamwork and cooperation can be fruitful most of the time. The youngster entrusted himself to the raven, the fish and the fox in turn, and achieved the almost impossible through learning stages.

How do the hiding places differ from each other? Twice, the raven and the fish extend shelter to the young man in a motherly and caring way, far removed from the king's daughter. What this old fairy tale mirrors is our unpleasant present-day reality. Technological surveillance methods have become so diverse that hardly any place still exists where one can remain undiscovered. Yet, the third hiding place is fundamentally different: after his transformation, the young man's appearance attracts the king's daughter. She shows interest in a living being and even wants to have it by her side, instead of staying alone. She allows the sea hare to cuddle up under her braid, whereas she does not allow anyone to come near her. As with other people who have a great fear of closeness and intimacy, her heart is moved by an animal to whom she can offer a relationship – the first ever. Her power and obsession to control have been disrupted.

When they both look out of the windows together at the end of the story, she cannot find the young man. She has no knowledge of her inner rooms and therefore, her emotional world. As long as she sees and controls others and knows how they are doing, she is unaware of herself and matters of the heart. And she was correct in her self-assessment: only if she had remained completely free, independent and entirely on her own, would she have retained universal oversight and the related power. She must also tolerate the king's secret, and because she is now capable of doing so, she has become capable of entering into and having a relationship. In relationships, secrets almost always exist and need to be kept, because we can never fully know ourselves, the other person, or the relationship itself. Something always remains unconscious.

Reading this fairy tale, who is not reminded of George Orwell's novel *1984*, published in 1949 and sketching a world of surveillance? Once the secret surveillance program of the US secret service NSA became known in June 2013, this book moved up to rank 66 in the USA and rank 42 in the British best-seller booklists of internet giant Amazon, and even topped the list in the USA at the end of January 2017. It would be misleading, though, to find surveillance methods only within state organizations and institutions. Many people have come to use surveillance systems quite naturally in their private lives. Network scanning is en vogue, accepted or even demanded. Psychologically speaking, surveillance has become a largely ego-syntonic phenomenon.

On the Difficulty of Trusting

Kerstin Kullmann addressed the impact of this trend in 2013 in an article subtitled "Fearing that their offspring might fail in life, parents are keeping a close watch over their children. Out of love, they control their children's school, study and career progress at close range. Whether these sheltered creatures will grow up to be happy adults is questionable." (Kullmann 2013*)

An increasing number of parents seems to be inordinately worried about their children, as witnessed by a student who experiences the effects of this mistrust firsthand through her work at the telephone hotline of a well-known university. She is responsible for explaining the details of application deadlines, any intended changes in subject matter of study and forthcoming university transfers to callers. She has recently noticed that every other phone call comes from a parent and, in most cases, they are well versed in the study programs which their children are pursuing. Their questions differ from the usual inquiries: parents want to know whether the application deadline that their child has given them is correct – these are calls of a controlling nature.

Trust grows with familiarity. The closer we are to a person, the more positively we experience each other, the more we trust. Trust can grow over time spent together. Trust exists as long as we are not being cheated or lied to, as long as we are not disappointed. Against this background, it may be surprising that parents react with such a high degree of suspicion. In fact, not only do they distrust their own children, whose weaknesses they are well aware of, but also teachers, institutions, God, fate and much more. This mistrust seems to be of a fundamental nature, affecting almost all areas of life. But when is control necessary and at what point does it become destructive? Trust in essence harbors risk, because we believe something instead of knowing it. Those who consciously trust, consciously renounce knowledge or control. As shown in the fairy tale, not knowing something in a relationship endows the other person with a secret. Someone who can tolerate secrets renounces power over others, at least partially, which is a prerequisite for respect and love. There is no love without trust. Hence, with dwindling trust, our ability to love will likewise dwindle. People who are capable of reflective trust – as opposed to blind or naive trust – recognize that others may sometimes be weak, unreliable or "evil", make mistakes and cannot consistently fulfil the trust placed in them, or might even abuse it at times. This is a painful experience.

In order to increase trust, we need to allow ourselves to be vulnerable. Vulnerability is the starting point for trust, which means we have to take risks – whoever shuns them seeks control. Trust is a strength which many of us would not want to live without. Why? If we control more than we trust, we start to suspect evil intentions, even in situations where there would be every reason to trust. The notion that others are incompetent, lazy, mean, unfaithful, disingenuous, criminal etc. becomes engrained in our minds and hearts as the norm. We begin to suspect and seek evil everywhere, and general suspicion becomes the rule. However, our view of reality will become distorted if we consistently seek that which is potentially bad. There is a saying that honest people have nothing to fear when they are controlled, but the fact still remains that their honesty must be proven in the first place. My assumption is that insinuation will ultimately increase that which we seek to weed out.

To make people more aware of the consequences of total control in human relationships – and at this point that is all we are talking about – it is worth taking a look at Dave

Eggers' novel *The Circle*. His work is considered the *1984* of the internet age and describes an internet society under full transparency and surveillance. The main character is 24-year-old Mae Holland, who is overjoyed to be starting her job at the globally dominant internet company Circle, a Californian enterprise run by its three founders. It quickly becomes clear that in the world of the Circle, secrets are considered a crime. Everything must be kept visible, which is why places and people all over the world are equipped with video cameras. Mae quickly becomes a model employee and enthusiastically promotes this total transparency. Nothing remains hidden anymore, everyone can observe everything that is happening. This concept promises equal rights, a world without murder, corruption, kidnapping, rape or abuse of power. Evil would no longer stand a chance. A former theology student sums this up as follows:

> Now all humans will have the eyes of God. [...] Now we're all God. Every one of us will soon be able to see, and cast judgment upon, every other. We'll see what He sees. (Eggers 2013, 398f.)

When one of the three founders of the Circle asks Mae if she can think of anyone who would want to be watched all the time, she answers: "I do. I want to be seen. I want proof I existed" (Eggers 2013, 490). This is no longer some remote idea, as sociologist Zygmunt Baumann points out – invisibility in the information age of today basically means death. He believes that people have some kind of unconscious longing to transform themselves into remarkable, desirable commodities which cannot be overlooked, abandoned or dismissed (Baumann 2009, 12).

Many people who have gained worldwide attention through their strong social media presence confirm that they in fact enjoy this kind of attention, especially when it makes them sought-after advertisers, or so-called influencers. Conversely, if you are invisible, you are degraded to being almost nothing. Could this phenomenon explain why so many people are adamant about taking part in TV shows today, although they run the risk of being put to shame? Shame is the ability to protect one's own intimacy and has to be suppressed if someone is eager to be visible.

Her fascination with transparency makes the novel's heroine Mae lose all respect for the human need for individual privacy and intimacy. Outraged by this behavior, her parents turn away from her. Mae also wants to prove to her former partner Mercer that no one can hide from the Circle nor are they allowed to do so, because everything private is considered as theft. Mae starts searching and hunting for Mercer, who has retreated into solitude in a remote area. When he realizes with horror that he cannot escape, he chooses to kill himself. Where darkness is eradicated, life becomes hell.

The Pastperfect project alluded to in the novel publishes data about people's ancestors and in this way, destroys Mae's best friend Annie. When she learns the truth about the atrocities committed by her ancestors and witnesses the reaction of her followers, Annie falls into a coma. In the final scene of the novel, Mae stands in front of Annie's bed and looks at the device monitoring her brain. Color explosions appear at regular intervals, showing her brain activity. Mae is annoyed because she cannot decipher these images and does not know what is going on in her friend's head. Although she touches Annie's forehead with her hand, an insurmountable distance remains between them. Mae's despair at not knowing what thoughts are concealed in Annie's head finally turn to anger. In the book's final scene, Mae decides to crack this mental secret.

Events from a few years back remind us that a desire for a better world may tempt us into accepting better surveillance measures: For many years, California suffered from catastrophic drought and water scarcity, so that farmers were confronted with significant losses, threatening many with insolvency. In May 2015, satellite images of the homes of world-famous stars came in handy: lush greenery in the gardens of Barbara Streisand, Kim Kardashian and others triggered a wave of indignation in social media. In fact, water consumption in the wealthy Beverly Hills' neighborhoods is three times higher than elsewhere, and this imbalance could no longer remain concealed thanks to the cameras. If the public learns about secret contracts, conversations or files, for example through Wikileaks, the image upheld by powerful people can be damaged, and abuse of power is impeded. Backroom politics have become riskier in a time when everything can be recorded on mobile phones.

But how far will we take surveillance for security reasons? The abduction and murder of Annelie, a 17-year-old girl from Saxony, in August 2015 raised this question for many parents. What can we do to prevent these crimes? Should we implant microchips in our children so that they can be located at any time? If we take such measures, our fears would win out at the expense of the freedom that every young person needs to become independent.

On 16 May 2015, the BBC reported that the government of South Korea had obliged parents to monitor their children online. Parents can access their children's smartphone with an app called Smart Sheriff and – so the government's idea – protect them from pornography and other dubious content on the internet. Security and the fight against evil are rational arguments in convincing skeptics to ultimately agree to surveillance options. The technology company Three

Square Market came up with a more cheerful idea. On 1 August 2017, they invited employees to a "chip party". 50 of the 80 staff members volunteered to have a chip the size of a rice grain implanted under their skin to make life easier. The little device enables coworkers to open doors, log onto their PC, make payments and much more (Astor 2017).

A comparison between the novel *The Circle* and the fairy tale *The Sea Hare* reveals opposing processes at work. Whereas in the fairy tale, the king's daughter becomes capable of engaging in a relationship by sacrificing her universal vision, in the novel, the heroine Mae gradually loses all her relationships and ends up completely alone. The more she can see and control, the lonelier she gets, and missing out on something makes her even more angry. Fascinated by the all-seeing eye, she is unaware of how inhumane it is to forbid any intimacy. This kind of terror looms whenever the ego presumes what was once the right of the gods. It is also worth noting that someone who would be able to see everything, would also be confronted with the world's most terrible injustice, cruelty and death.

The protagonist Will Salas in the film *In Time* asks his attractive lover Sylvia how the so-called responsible elite can bear such suffering. As a member of the upper class, Sylvia has an easy solution: "You simply look away, you close your eyes." In other words, we only want to see what is beautiful.

On the Nature of Beauty

In 1927, Jung declared (Jung 1969, CW 8, §707) that human life without beauty would be dull beyond all measure. Indeed, beauty enriches our lives in many ways. When we look at nature, we are amazed at the veritable explosion of beauty that unfolds before our eyes. Just consider the magnificent fan of a peacock, a sunset, a mountain peak, the night sky, snow crystals on the windowpane or the coils of the shell of a sea snail. The latter was described by Italian mathematician Leonardo Fibonacci after whom the formula was named. The Fibonacci formula and the so-called "Golden Ratio"[11], as well as the geometry of a snow crystal, illustrate that beauty can be described in mathematical terms. Beauty is not chaos, but instead follows a harmonious order, an exact structure and objective universal laws. If it were dark or if we did not have eyes, this beauty would pass us by unawares.[12] It may be surprising to learn that women and men with average-looking faces are perceived as particularly attractive. As early as 1990, US psychologists Judith Langlois and Lori Roggman proved this to be the case by digitally mixing a large number of photos of faces. The resulting symmetrical and well-proportioned average faces were found particularly appealing by test persons. In this context, "average" refers to ears that do not stick out too much, large eyes, full lips, a high forehead and a smooth and evenly colored skin. Such an average face is, however, unusually well shaped and evenly balanced, which makes it quite rare (Hollersen 2014).

Youth is one important beauty factor that must not be forgotten. On average, women in their early twenties are sexually most attractive to men of all ages. Childlike facial features are desirable, which is why age, as we all know, is physical beauty's greatest enemy. Despite medical intervention, our

---

11. Around the year 1200, Fibonacci described growth processes with the sequence $F_n=F_{n-1}+F_{n-2}$ for n > 2 : 1, 2, 3, 5, 8, 13, 21, etc.
   The formula for the Golden Ratio is $a/b = (a + b)/a = 1,618...$
   The navel divides our body according to the Golden Ratio.
12. Beauty can still be perceived without eyes, for example in music.

physical beauty is short-lived and something we cannot really hold on to.

In one of his novels, Martin Walser hits the nerve of the present day when he remarks: "There is nothing that is more than beautiful. To be beautiful, then, is the utmost we can ever hope to achieve" (Walser 2016, 7 and 9 *). As one of the highest commodities, beauty has something divine to it from a psychological point of view, namely a share of the self. We find indications of this notion in the Kabbalah Tree of Life, with the underlying idea that the fullness of the one God radiates into the world in various facets. And the Sephiroth Tipheret as the sixth of ten emanations of God – and thus the sixth quality through which God flows into the world – embodies nothing less than beauty combined with splendor, glory and magnificence. The concept of beauty as one of the ultimate values residing or originating in God is also known in other religious traditions. The reference to the sun's radiance in the Vedic Brahman is a parallel to Yahweh's glory of light. And Mohammed says: "God is beauty and loves beauty" (Heiler 1979, 462).

The more we optimize ourselves in this respect, the more we can participate in divine beauty. What is the effect of beauty? Stendhal (quoted from Liessmann 2009, 8) says that it promises, yet does not guarantee happiness. This is also reflected in Greek mythology, e.g. when Eris, the goddess of discord, once threw an apple at Mount Olympus, and a dispute ensued over who was the most beautiful goddess. Zeus, wise as he was, did not want to answer this question and therefore sent the gods' messenger Hermes to Paris, son of the Trojan king, to make the choice and bear the consequences. All three rival goddesses – Hera, Athena and Aphrodite – tried to bribe Paris. Hera, the wife of Zeus, offered Paris power in return for being elected the most beautiful goddess. Athena promised him wisdom and the art of war if he named her, and Aphrodite wanted to give him Helen, the most beautiful woman in the world at that time. That's when Paris took the bait: it was the greatest temptation to own the most beautiful woman. Hence, Eris was successful, for Paris' decision not only heightened the rivalry between the three goddesses, but also triggered the Trojan War, which was perhaps the first major East-West conflict. Under certain circumstances, beauty can therefore be said to bring something destructive in its train, which Rainer Maria Rilke expresses in the first Duino Elegy as follows: "For beauty is nothing but the beginning of terror" (Rilke 2009, 3).

But firstly, beauty brings many advantages. It is proven that attractive people receive preferential treatment at the supermarket counter, during exams, in court and in many other situations. Even when cheating at school or fare dodging on public transport, beautiful people are said to be let off more easily if they get caught. It could be that we make this assumption because we are unconsciously suspicious of beauty. Back in ancient times, beautiful people were seen to represent the good, the true and the pure, and were considered noble, healthy and strong. Such projections of beauty are still effective today. A noble soul is assumed to exist in a beautiful body, to the extent that external and internal beauty are often considered to be one and the same thing (Liessmann 2009, 16 and 93). Another effect which beauty has was demonstrated in a simple experiment conducted by Ernst Roidl (Huf 2013, 127f) who investigated for how long men can keep their hands in cold water. Eleven men received instructions from a woman who wore makeup and sexy clothes. Eleven further men were admitted to this trial by the same woman, only this time, she had no make-up on and wore a lab coat. The results are hardly surprising: The men in the first group were able to keep their hands in cold water for twice as long as the men in the second group. In the presence of a beautiful woman, men will try harder and perform better.

It thus seems that beauty is highly effective, and it is not surprising to learn that extremely attractive women are more troubled by aging, because they have a lot to lose. They do not exactly become ugly, but simply less attractive, inconspicuous and less noticeable than in younger years. Arnon Grünberg describes the consequences as follows:

The most beautiful thing in the world is to be desired. [...] Everything revolves around being desired, and all pain begins where desire ends. (Grünberg 2006, 57*)

It hurts to be less desirable and results in a changed relationship with others and oneself, because beauty is something of such value and impact that its loss is difficult to bear.

Beauty is in the Eye of the Beholder and the Respective (Sub-) Culture

Human beauty is so much more than a natural, evenly shaped face or body. In no era has an ideal natural body that has not needed to conform to culturally determined modifications in the name of beauty ever existed. Beauty was and is embedded in cultural and religious ideas.

The voluptuous female bodies depicted in Rubens' paintings in the 17th century are now considered to be unaesthetically corpulent, and the lip plates of women in Ethiopia or lotus feet of Chinese women do not have any aesthetic value in today's Western world. The feet of young girls were bandaged tightly at the early age of around five and the toes usually broken in the process in order to achieve lotus feet. The target was a shoe size between 2 and 6.4 US size, i.e. the size of small children's feet. Most probably, these feet served as a target for projection in the sense that women with such feet were regarded as cute, delicate and weak. In any case, they were considered to be morally superior because they hardly ever came into contact with the dirt on the ground. Farmers' wives could not be allowed to have such dainty feet, with which only little steps could be taken, as work in the field and the house would not have been manageable. Lotus feet were therefore only affordable for rich people who did not have to work. This phenomenon still holds value today: beauty opens the door to a higher social class.

Lip plates or lotus feet also illustrate that cruelty, mutilation and illness have long been part of the human concept of beauty. The same holds true for anorexia. What medicine defines as an illness serves as a beauty ideal for anorexic people. Yet, a changing beauty ideal can trigger a healing process – on the collective and the individual level. As an example, 17-year-old anorexic Laura describes how she happened to become aware of an extremely thin, anorexic woman one day. Her rickety legs, tired eyes and empty facial expression affected her deeply. All of a sudden, Laura could no longer perceive such a body as beautiful and enviable and did not want to end up looking like that. This sudden realization enabled her to let go of anorexia and its ideals, and to finally become healthy again. Hence, beauty also lies in the eye of the beholder.

The link between illness and beauty is also evident on the catwalks around the globe: Model Winnie Harlow suffers from vitiligo and her colleague Thando Hopa from albinism.[13] The rare conditions both women suffer from and their distinctive features make them attractive for the Western market. This again shows that beauty needs well-dosed dissonance. Where previously the beauty spot reigned, an ailment can now be fortuitous, if it manifests itself in an otherwise perfect body, as seen in the likes of Winnie Harlow or Thanda Hopa. That little bit of extra originality is needed to make someone noticeable. Uniqueness and distinctiveness are required to stand out from the crowd, attracting the attention that is ultimately at stake.

Beauty is no longer in as short supply today as it was in the Middle Ages. Many more people can afford to improve their looks, therefore, one needs something out of the ordinary as a contrast to the average manufactured beauty.

The more than 2000-year-old fairy tale of Amor and Psyche deals with the possible consequences of extraordinary beauty. Psyche is the youngest of a royal couple's three daughters and is exceptionally beautiful. Her two older sisters are also very beautiful, but not as beautiful as Psyche, who is admired and even adulated by many men. But in contrast to her two sisters, not a single suitor asks for Psyche's hand. How can that be? Psyche experiences herself as a mere object of men's marvel and admiration. No man dares to come closer or fall in love with her. Psyche suffers bitterly from her loneliness and begins to hate herself and her body. The fairy tale tells us that self-hate and loneliness are ancient phenomena which can also befall very beautiful people or hit extremely beautiful people especially hard. Psyche perceives her divine beauty almost as

---

13. As a child, Willie Harlow was mocked as a zebra and cow because of her vitiligo. Thando Hopa points out that people suffering from albinism are still being threatened or expelled from communities in East Africa today. In 2015, four men in Tanzania were convicted of killing a man suffering from albinism in order to sell his body parts for their alleged magical powers (Lauer 2015; Putsch 2015).

a curse, because it seems to be the reason why she becomes an object on display or a showpiece. Her perfect beauty appears to be an obstacle to experiencing relationships and love. In view of the articles we read about famous beautiful people in the tabloid press, it is evident that this fairy tale reflects a timeless reality.

The biography of American Cindy Jackson also follows this fairytale pattern. From her earliest youth, she hated her heavily built body and therefore underwent no less than 52 cosmetic surgery procedures to remodel it from head to toe. She finally achieved her desired Barbie doll appearance (www. cindyjackson.com). In the course of many years of surgical remodeling, she became gradually more beautiful, but also lonelier than ever. Her love affairs lasted less and less over time, until only a platonic companion was left to her. Her desire for biological children also diminished, as pregnancy would have destroyed the body opus she had created, which she did not want to risk. Change is the enemy of perfect beauty, because every change can only be for the worse.

Beauty is no longer God-given, but Hard Work

Helena Rubinstein allegedly once said: "There are no ugly women, only lazy ones." This statement hits the right note in the present world, where the ego rather than our biological fate has become increasingly responsible for beauty. The ego needs discipline, time, money and a good surgeon to improve its own beauty. In this context, many people view beauty not just as hard work, but as a duty if they want to survive in today's job or relationship market. We are judged on a physical level and our external appearance determines our social and economic status. Siegfried Kracauer observed this phenomenon as early as the end of the 1920s. In his opinion, the reason why people visited beauty salons was not so much a penchant for luxury as an expression of existential worry. The fear of being withdrawn from the market began to spread (Baumann 2009, 7). The fact that today's competition can hardly be won without body shaping or enhancement is probably also true for politicians. Austrian youth researcher Bernhard Heinzlmaier confirms the power of optics: According to his surveys, aesthetic characteristics have become very important to young voters. The ideal type of politician is the "slim-fit warrior" (dpa, 11 August 2017).

Because the "right", i.e. beautiful, body pays off, plastic surgeons are being consulted at an increased rate by both women and men. To condemn such cosmetic surgery as decadent seems inappropriate to French artist Orlan: "It seems really strange to me to condemn a woman and find it untenable if she does not accept herself as she is. It's anachronistic. After all, people also have artificial teeth, artificial hip or knee joints or a pacemaker. It's socially acceptable." (Meister 2013 *)

As a representative of so-called Body Art, Orlan has altered her body with cosmetic surgery since 1978 and has demanded the freedom to shape one's own body (www.orlan.eu). In the process, she also wanted procedures beyond the usual beauty ideology to be carried out on her, for example, having two silicone implants attached to her forehead. It is interesting to note that male surgeons have rejected such requests, pointing out that no man would want to sleep with her voluntarily with such a disfigured face. Through her work, Orlan wants to draw our attention to beauty ideals that imprison us because they deny us the freedom to deviate from collective norms: It is only when we perceive this pressure for standardization that we can decide whether to accept or reject such beauty concepts. This is also pointed out by British psychoanalyst Susie Orbach (Orbach 2009). Although a beautiful body and the pursuit of its perfection have been democratized, the concept of beauty is not based on aesthetic diversity, but on very strict beauty standards that result in beauty terror.

Beauty in Psychotherapeutic Practice

According to Susie Orbach (Orbach 2009, 6), beauty is becoming an increasingly important topic in psychotherapy, because current cultural conventions lead to a destabilization of our bodies with increasing discomfort and insecurity. The consequences are permanently anxious self-observation and self-control. Controlling and shaping the body according to the collective ideal has become an obsession for many. A healthy and beautiful body seems to have turned into a moral obligation for millions of people: almost everywhere, being fat is considered repulsive and an expression of weakness, while being slim is considered good. Those who fail to comply with the shedding of excess pounds experience shame or guilt.

But nowadays, even people of normal weight struggle to determine what they are still allowed to eat, what is dangerous and what is taboo. Eating a piece of cream cake is even referred to as "sinning".

Food taboos have been part of religion as long as anyone can remember. In today's Western world, fewer and fewer people are following the dietary rules laid down by the Christian church, voluntarily restricting themselves and choosing to become vegetarians, vegans, frutarians, freegans and the like – an expression of plurality and individuality.

Since food commandments have always existed, they are probably a primeval human need, an archetypal necessity, which we morally justify to prove ourselves religious. This becomes particularly obvious when modern eating commandments are accompanied by either a fanatic sense of superiority or an irrational fear of certain food components. Terms such as "orthorexia" – an inner compulsion to eat only healthy food – or more benevolent sounding terms like "clean eating" or "detox food" bear witness to this trend.

Abstaining from food and fasting are part of Christian tradition. With the general spread of Christianity, the triumphant march of asceticism began, which is generally found wherever basic instincts are strong, and nature and naturalness become frightening to the extent that they must be throttled (Jung 1956, CW 5, §120). Attempts to tame the body, even if they now come in modern guise, are old and religiously founded human endeavors.

Transference and Countertransference of Beauty

What happens when an extremely good-looking patient enters a psychotherapeutic practice? It is unlikely to remain without effect. Perhaps our body response makes us feel more uncomfortable or insecure than usual. Perhaps we choose to dress up for the sessions more consciously. The need to appear more attractive, envy or erotic feelings can surface – and are suppressed. Conversely, what kind of influence would a physically very attractive therapist exert on the course of treatment? How do patients and therapists deal with their respective feelings of envy or admiration? Addressing such questions can lead to greater awareness of one's own relationship to beauty.

Therapists might become conscious of the fact that they prefer patients to resolve dissatisfaction with their bodies on a psychological level by accepting their physical appearance as it is. Sometimes, an unconscious envy of what is possible with the help of cosmetic surgery is hidden behind such desires.

It would be only too easy for psychotherapy to label people who avail themselves of plastic surgery or are even addicted to it as vain or pathologic. Susie Orbach does not always find it appropriate to look for the roots of suffering in the psyche, for the body is not merely a background actor or valet. Orbach tells the story of a man who put both his legs in dry ice to deaden them and how the resulting amputation brought him a level of satisfaction he had never known before. The reason for his satisfaction was that his damaged body now mirrored his emotional damage – inner and outer reality had become congruent (Orbach 2009, 15). This certainly extreme case shows that even a "defective" or surgically altered body can provide the stability of an anchor and a feeling of being comfortable with one's body. Finally, this example also confronts us with the primeval human need to modify the body which nature has given us. As long as this happens within the limits of a collective trend, questions are rarely raised. In contrast, accommodating an individual's unique request is often perceived as bizarre or abnormal, which only shows the extent to which we are influenced by convention.

5. The Dark Self

Christ as a Self-Symbol?

Anything that a man postulates as being a greater totality than himself can become a symbol of the self. For this reason, the symbol of the self is not always as total as the definition would require. Even the Christ-figure is not a totality, for it lacks the nocturnal side of the psyche's nature, the darkness of the spirit, and is also without sin. Without the integration of evil there is no totality [...].
(Jung 1958, CW 11, §232)

In assuming that the self cannot only be good, positive and radiantly bright, because we require a dark side to be complete, we should not necessarily have to think of the devil as one and Christ as the other half of the self. Painful, destructive, even unfathomable things can certainly be found in Christ: for example, the stations of the cross, his rather cruel death on the cross and his complete abandonment by God (deus absconditus) in death are "inhumane" situations, exposing the Father in heaven as "evil". Whether we seek to find the shadow side of the self in the devil, or darkness in Christ and God, the logical consequences are quite brutal:

> So too the self is our life's goal, for it is the completest expression of that fateful combination we call individuality [...]. (Jung 1966, CW 7, §404)

and

> And because individuation is an heroic and often tragic task, the most difficult of all, it involves suffering, a passion of the ego: the ordinary, empirical man we once were is burdened with the fate of losing himself in a greater dimension and being robbed of his fancied freedom of will. He suffers, so to speak, from the violence done to him by the self. (Jung 1958, CW 11, §233)

If the realization of the self is the central goal of individuation, then inevitably, the dark God will also be realized – sometimes against the will of the ego. Then bestial, malicious, destructive and criminal elements, as well as suffering will have a place in personality development. This thought is unpleasant, but part of the reality of life. Besides, any attempts to realize only the bright side have failed to this day. In the past, there have been quite a few role models whose dark self has remained hidden behind a charismatic aura for a long time only to surface from the depths of the abyss and become visible at some point in their lives to the disbelief of their contemporaries. Charisma can disguise the shadow and tempt others to project overly positive aspects onto a person.

One area of life where the dark self may present itself is sexuality. According to Peer Hultberg (Hultberg 2009, 217ff), the sadomasochistic elements of Christ's Passion could lead us to an understanding of sadomasochism as a relationship between the ego and the dark self. For Hultberg, sadomasochism is a human longing for a union with the dark chthonic God, dwelling in matter, and sexual ecstasy in sadomasochism could be interpreted as a highly unconscious modern experience of God. We see certain parallels in ancient initiation rites, whose sadomasochistic elements confronted initiates with the darker destructive side of higher powers.

Hultberg substantiates his hypothesis with the *Story of O.*, in which an intellectually and emotionally highly differentiated woman embarks on a search for ego-transcending experience. She seeks God in the sexual realm, as he can only be found by experiencing extremes. For this purpose, O. has herself abducted to a remote castle in order to completely submit herself to a group of men. She is regularly brought to her masters to serve them. Back in her normal everyday life, O. feels inspired and full of energy. After another experience in the service of a woman, O. experiences an intense feeling of liberation and vitality. In her ecstatic experiences, she encounters the dark God in male and female form and has the feeling of being reborn.

The unbroken fascination for sadomasochism is evident in the sales records of *Fifty Shades of Grey*, a trilogy of novels by British author E. L. James. More than 100 million copies have been sold worldwide and the first of the three novels is considered the fastest selling paperback of all time in the United Kingdom.

In 1974, artist Marina Abramovic demonstrated what voluntarily offering complete control over one's body might result in, i.e. if like O. one is prepared to give oneself completely to others.

In a performance titled *Rhythm 0*, she physically exposed herself to her audience for six hours, taking full responsibility for the outcome (Vorkoeper 2006). She had placed carefully selected objects on a table which spectators could use to give her either pain or pleasure, while she remained passive. It is known that after three hours, the situation appeared to be out of control and the police had to be called in because the artist was already half-naked and wounded. In 2016, Marina Abramovic reported that she needed 30 years after the event before she could allow others to do something to her body again.

Voluntary submission does not necessarily lead to ecstasy, as with O., but can result in a severe trauma. In situations of abuse or sexual assault, which are not voluntary, but carried out under duress, severe trauma is the rule. A sexual assault can be a terribly distressing experience, but it can also be a numinous one – still, it is of a destructive nature. An example is a 30-year-old female patient, who cannot speak about her abuse at the hands of her older brother without feeling that she is losing herself. Her ego-complex is massively shaken by these memories to the point of fragmentation. On a rational level, many people do not understand this, and neither why victims do not end their suffering by breaking their silence at an earlier stage. Apart from the fact that perpetrators often silence their victims with threats, the ego is usually robbed of freedom on the archetypal level. In encountering the self, the ego loses much, sometimes its entire freedom, as mentioned above by Jung. An ego overwhelmed to this extent is no longer able to say "no" or "stop".

In this context, it becomes clear that the collective trend towards an abstract image of God – as depicted above – cannot be entirely correct. If God is sought in sexuality, then he is sought in the sensual and material realm. Even physicists suspect something divine in matter when referring to the so-called Higgs particle as the particle of God – even if this is meant somewhat flippantly. Locating the divine in matter is a rather old idea, also adopted by Jung. In his opinion, the self is mysteriously rooted in the darkness of matter (Jung 1959, CW 9/1, §291).

Cannibalism

On 29 March 2001 (Knobbe & Schmalenberg 2003), Bernd B. drove to see Armin M., whom he had met on the internet under the alias "antrophagus". After the death of his mother, Armin M. had had two basement rooms built in his courtyard, one of which was in the guise of a slaughter room equipped with a video camera. In front of a running camera, Bernd B. undressed himself and had his penis cut off by Armin M. After the wound had been professionally dressed, the two men together ate Bernd's manhood. Afterwards, Armin M. filmed himself killing his victim by stabbing and slashing him and then dissecting the corpse. He packed the flesh in portions in the freezer and buried some of the bones in the garden. After the killing of Bernd B., other men contacted Armin M., desiring to be slaughtered by him or to be eaten whilst still alive. And in January 2017, the public prosecutor in Nuremberg launched investigations against a 42-year-old man who had been seeking women for dismemberment and consumption in internet fora.

Whosoever is vexed by such activities shall be reminded that the Gospel of John reads:

> Jesus said to them: Amen, amen, I say to you: unless you eat the flesh of the Son of Man and drink his blood, you do not have life within you. Whoever eats my flesh and drinks my blood has eternal life and I will raise him on the last day. For my flesh is true food and my blood is true drink. Whoever eats my flesh and drinks my blood remains in me, and I in him. (John 6, 53-56)

Whosoever claims that this biblical statement must be understood symbolically, cannot fail to recognize its cannibalistic connotation. Moreover, in a Catholic Mass, a host is eaten in the conviction that the body of Christ is represented in a substantial and not merely a symbolical manner.

The killing of Bernd B. reminds us of the visions of Zosimos of Panopolis, a natural philosopher and alchemist of the 3rd century, whose work is preserved in the famous alchemical Codex Marcianus (Jung 1959, CW 11, §403f). Some elements of his visions are replicated in the killing of Bernd B.:

1. The actors are two priests.
2. One priest slaughters the other.
3. The victim sacrifices himself voluntarily.
4. The sacrificial death is excruciating.
5. A dismemberment of the victim occurs.
6. The priest eats his own flesh.

The analogy between Zosimos' vision and cannibalistic activity could mean that God is revived on an unconscious level, with the aim of sacrifice, rupture, transformation and rebirth. Two further examples are the Greek god Dionysus and the Egyptian god Osiris (Jung 1967, CW 13, §91f). Psychologically speaking, cannibalism would represent an unconscious return of these repressed gods.

Bernd B. and Armin M. lived out an archetypal fantasy. In their search for vitality, it is most likely that they unconsciously sacrificed a life and in doing so, became victims themselves, or better yet – the plaything of archetypal powers. As a matter of fact, modern human beings do not act only in a reasonable and enlightened manner, and Jung's following statement is still valid:

In fairness to the primitive psyche, however, I would like to emphasize that the "holy dread" of civilized man differs but little from the awe of the primitive, and that the God who is present and active in the mystery is a mystery for both (Jung 1959, CW 11, §375)

Perhaps people who are repelled by the banality and sterility of life are particularly vulnerable when it comes to committing such unfathomable acts. In a world that is constantly striving for purity, beauty and goodness to eradicate the shadow side of things, it would increasingly appear that a compensatory longing for dark rites exists. In view of the fact that the world is becoming ever more "desensualized", it is precisely this sensuality that is fascinating.

The attractive proposition of committing the unfathomable to compensate for unbearable beauty appears in Arnon Grünberg's novel *Gnadenfrist*:

Sometimes, everything is so beautiful, so terribly beautiful, so unbearably beautiful, that Warnke pictures himself drowning his two daughters like two young kittens in a burlap sack with stones. (Grünberg 2006, 34*)

and

Warnke is digging in the ground, thinking of his daughters, but no matter how much effort he puts into thinking about something else, something cheerful and innocent, he can only picture himself putting them in a large burlap sack, like the one lying around somewhere in the basement of his house as a Santa Claus accessory, and weighing the bag down with stones. (Grünberg 2006, 74*)

Perversity is an experience in which dark numinous forces pressure the ego into its service. Even the most indecent proposals to be found on the internet do not herald our arrival in a "new dimension", as the headline on a magazine cover once suggested. Archetypes still have the same effect as always, although this sometimes goes unnoticed. They operate beyond moral categories, which is why all facets of the self, both destructive and beneficial, exude an unwavering fascination.

In a milder form, the longing for numinous horror appears in so-called disaster tourism (Vidal-Folch 2015): A former Latvian prison, for example, offers tourists the "full prison experience" with overnight accommodation in a cell, including death threats, the sound of machine gunfire and screams from adjacent cells. An escape attempt can be booked as an extra, during which numerous obstacles and surveillance cameras must be overcome in order to regain freedom. Another example is Sichuan in southern China, which was hit by an earthquake in 2008. Billboards advertising a tour of the city's ruins read: "Come and discover the areas devastated by one of the deadliest earthquakes in recent history". This type of tourism allowing people to follow the trail of horror caused by human barbarity or natural disaster is referred to as "dark tourism". The Grimm fairy tale *The Story of the Youth Who Went Forth to Learn What Fear Was* also describes a similar search. Because the young protagonist finds that horror does not move him emotionally, he wants to learn more about it, and this topic would appear relevant to this day. Back in the 17th and 18th centuries, many people were still afraid of going up into the mountains or being in cemeteries, especially at nighttime, as these were eerie, dangerous places where someone would hardly choose to linger. The era of Enlightenment in the 18th century brought fundamental changes in this respect. One of the first testimonials of this was Jean-Jaques Rousseau, who liked to stand at the edge of an alpine gorge secured by a railing. "I love these vertigoes very much, provided that I am safe," he wrote (Giegerich 1988, 35). Having the creeps is a tingling, invigorating experience, but should not entail any danger. Rousseau was thus a pioneer of modern adventure tours, such as bungee jumping or river rafting, where safety is of utmost priority.

Emptiness

What happens if God projections result in emptiness, i.e. if it turns out that God is dead, non-existent or "completely absent"? At this point, the spiritual afterlife dissolves. The world as we know it, divided into this world and the next, loses the hereafter, along with paradise and hell, or the underworld. The only thing remaining is the mortal world. According to Heidegger (Lesmeister 2009, 60f), this should not be confused with an atheistic attitude. It means rather that the supersensible world of ideas, the spiritual world – also the Platonic triad of truth, beauty and goodness – has served its time as the foundation of earthly life and lost its supporting and energizing impact. Humans no longer have anything to hold on to, and are confronted with a metaphysical groundlessness, which, according to Lesmeister, does not lead to a disappearance, but rather to a re-allocation of values. New projections lead to pluralism, equality and indifference.

Whoever tries to picture nothing, inevitably fails, as every thought is already something. On this note, Heidegger emphasized that one cannot conceive of nothing with images or thoughts, but rather through boredom and, above all, through fear, since being slips away in fear (Lesmeister 2009, 63). The loss of being tempts us to use defense mechanisms, as pointed out by Danish author Janne Teller in her novel *Nothing*. When it was published in her home country, the book caused a scandal and was temporarily banned from Danish schools.

About the content: In the school of a fictitious small Danish town, student Pierre Anthon one day announces that since nothing is of any importance, it is not worth doing anything. As a consequence, he leaves the classroom and quits school. Agnes, his classmate and narrator of the story, feels great anxiety well up inside her. Pierre Anthon then climbs into a big old plum tree. From up above, he teases and provokes his classmates:

> "It's all a waste of time," he yelled one day. "Everything begins only to end." [...] It's all a big masquerade, all make-believe and making out you are the best at it. (Teller 2014, 8)

His classmates realize that they do not want to live in Pierre Anthon's world, and decide to get him to come down from the plum tree. They debate whether beating, praying or a complaint to the principal could be helpful. Finally, they start throwing stones at Pierre Anthon, who with his razor-sharp mind realizes that his schoolmates want to get him to come down because they are afraid of nothingness:

> But you'll find out you're a clown in a trivial circus where everyone tries to convince each other how vital it is to have a certain look one year and another the next. And then you'll find out that fame and the big wide world are outside of you, and inside there's nothing, and always will be, no matter what you do. [...] Why not admit from the outset that nothing matters and just enjoy the nothing that is? (Teller 2014, 28)

After this provocation, the children decide to prove to Pierre Anthon that there is something meaningful. They secretly collect a "pile of meaning" towards this end in a disused saw-mill: Each child has to give up something of personal value and is then allowed to decide who is next and what sacrifice they have to make. First of all, materially replaceable items, such as a fishing rod, a black football, earrings or a telescope, must be handed in. This process quickly triggers a spiral of psychological violence: the more painful one considers one's own sacrifice, the more extreme the sacrifice demanded of the next in line. The justification for these demands is that a particularly painful sacrifice is also of particular significance and meaning. Gerda has to add her beloved hamster to the pile, devoted Muslim Hussein his prayer rug, pious Kai the crucifix from the church, Elise the coffin with her recently deceased younger brother, Sofie her virginity and Rosa the life of a stray dog. Rosa then demands Jan-Johan's right index finger, because it probably played a special role when Sophie's virginity was "sacrificed". After Jan-Johan's finger is cut off, he reveals the project to the police and the public. Once people become aware of what is going on, the initial outcry of the parents leads to a worldwide media fuss about the "pile of meaning". For three and a half million dollars, an American museum eventually buys the pile, which has in the meantime become a work of art signifying the meaning and purpose of life. The children become famous and everyone is impressed, except Pierre Anthon. He sees the rapidly subsiding media hype as a proof of insignificance:

> Meaning is meaning. So if you really had found the mean-ing, you'd still have it. And the world's press would still be here trying to figure out what it was you'd found. But they are not, so whatever it was you found, it wasn't the meaning, because the meaning doesn't exist! (Teller 2014, 190f)

Pierre Anthon refers to the pile, which has cost his class-mates so much, as "garbage" and provokes the group by asking them why they sold the items that supposedly mean so much to them for money. When the children realize that their sacrifices have been in vain, they begin to beat each other up, full of anger over what they have done to each other. In the end, the group achieves its original goal: Pierre Anthon climbs down from the tree and joins them in the sawmill. He looks at the individual objects on the "pile of meaning" and wants to know, among other things, what the purpose of the little bloodstained scrap is. Sofie yells at him, because the bit of cloth proves that she has sacrificed her virginity. The item is of great importance to her. Furious, Pierre Anthon grabs Sofie and asks:

> And that's why you sold it? [...] If that kind of garbage ever meant anything at all, it stopped the day you sold it for money. (Teller 2014, 213)

Pierre Anthon asks them one by one what price they paid for the beloved hamster, for the prayer rug denoting practice of faith, for the flag as a symbol of patriotism, and so on. Finally, he asks Sofie: "And what is left to you if you have sold yourself? If it ever meant anything to you at all, you would never have sold it." Everyone remains silent, some cry, some lower their heads. They realize that Pierre Anthon has won his point. When he turns his back on them as he walks away, the classmates vent their joint hatred at him and beat him up until he lies motionless and cruelly battered next to the "pile of meaning". That same night, the sawmill burns down and with it the pile, and Pierre Anthon dies. He has not only taken the "pile of meaning" away from them, but meaning in general. It is all his fault. It is his fault that they have lost their desire for life and for the future. After this night, the classmates avoid any contact with each other. Severely traumatized Sofie is admitted to a mental health facility. Here's where the story ends.

Pierre Anthon puts an end to everyday life. Shaman-like, he leaves the group and retreats up a tree to devote himself to spiritual questions. His idea that nothing has any meaning radically devalues existence and the outside world. In questioning common collective goals and convictions, he confronts the class with the absurdity of our way of life. As Lesmeister (2009) points out, everything is of equal value, which at this point has a negative connotation. Existence is pointless, action is pointless, learning is pointless. The class experiences exactly what Heidegger described. The narrator and the entire group are afraid of nothingness and the loss of meaning. So great is their fear, so unbearable that it must be fought off or eliminated. And it was probably the same fear that had the decision-makers in its grips to the extent that they banned the book for a certain period and labelled it as taboo.

The classmates have to undertake something because they do not want to live, and probably cannot accept life, in Pierre Anthon's world. For the class, meaning and a purpose are essential for survival, which is why they want to destroy Pierre Anthon's spiritual worldview. In the end, the only way to silence him is by killing him. The novel shows how controversial and earnest the question of existence and meaning is. It demonstrates in a clear and comprehensible manner how brutal the reaction of people can be when they are robbed of their spiritual values. A sense of unendurable meaninglessness is the breeding ground for hatred and violence.

Unconsciously, inevitably and pretty soon, the classmates' search for meaning leads to the exposure of their dark self: the futile attempts at avoiding a sacrifice, despair over their loss,

the killing of a dog, the severance of a finger, blasphemous sacrifices and the deflowering of Sofie, who becomes psychotic,
all bear witness to this. The search for meaning leads directly
to the edge of or into the depths of the abyss. The novel
also describes how meaning experienced subjectively can be
turned into collective meaning by selling it. Something that is
valuable on the subjective level becomes collectively valuable
by attributing a monetary value to it. The collective offers
meaning to those seeking it. That which has meaning can
now be publicly exhibited, aestheticized, marveled at, gazed
at, and admired – from a safe distance, comparable to the
railing which protected Rousseau from falling.

Sacrificing and selling a bicycle, football or sandals may be
bearable, as the individuals concerned may even make a bar-
gain from their sale and achieve added value. But what if the
beloved hamster, the belief in God, the fatherland, or sexual
virginity are sold? How can this be coped with emotionally?
Feelings of emptiness, pain or despair linger on.

The novel reveals two further essential issues: Shortly
before his death, Pierre Anthon becomes very angry, which
proves that he does care after all. He feels very bad that his
classmates have sold the "pile of meaning", their valuables and
themselves in the process. He denounces this as it touches him
and evokes strong feelings. By showing anger, Pierre Anthon
proves that he is aware of values, as we all are, and that being,
purpose and meaning do in fact exist – despite nothingness.

Friedrich Weinreb once said that man is God's counterpart, whereby the counterpart is the exact opposite of that
which constitutes human existence. Hence, if this world is all
about the tangible, then the opposite is the intangible up to a
point where we feel a boundless emptiness or nothing. Nothing is also a counterpart – as something completely different.
Moreover, the Hebrew word "nothing" is written in the same

letters as the word "I". The German word "ich" (I) is also contained in the German "nichts" (nothing), quasi embedded in or embraced by it (Weinreb 2002, 11). Weinreb describes nothing as the counterpart of existence. This nothing can be God, and humans may venture into a relationship with it.

Pierre Anthon stresses the tension between an internal emptiness and external fame and success. But despite this emptiness, he does not sit in the tree to display an entirely nihilistic attitude – he pleads that it be enjoyed. He contemplates the sky, while he practices getting used to doing nothing (Teller 2014, 9). His contemplative life, his pondering about the absurdity of life need not lead to profound despair, but can paradoxically be experienced as fullness, too. Nothing is not solely terrifying, but also pleasing. The rest of the class labels this attitude as diabolical, which it certainly is from a capitalist perspective.

The Dark Self in Therapy

According to Francoise O'Kane, the dark self is mostly avoided in therapeutic work. Without even the tiniest margin of progress or no possibility of conquering the dark, either as a hero, trickster, or through identification/inflation or other means, for those who cannot ward off their dark self, only encounter with it remains. The ego is then able to endure the presence of the dark self, can bear it, go along with it, be a witness of or know it (O'Kane 1993, 49ff). O'Kane talks about becoming familiar with the dark self and recalls an Eskimo ritual that consciously seeks this experience. To this end, Eskimos must seek solitude to throw off the trappings of everyday life, the familiar, the community and the security that all of this relates to. As a first step, they come into contact with nature and have to endure hunger and cold. After a few weeks of privation, they reach the second step, the goal of which is to "see your own skeleton and name each bone in ritual language". Eskimos monotonously and patiently rub two stones together until they see themselves stripped of their clothes and flesh. Upon perceiving their skeleton, they encounter an inner light and magic fire. This is the immortal soul of life – the self. This ritual also demonstrates what it means to advance to the eternal spirit, which leaves the flesh – the material realm – behind. This experience is only possible when humans are close to death. Stripping down to the bones is an image of the nothingness in this earthly world.

O'Kane does not deem it necessary to spare patients from all suffering, which is why analysis can also be hell, metaphorically speaking. But people should not suffer more discomfort than necessary, and identifying with the role of the victim prevents the experience of one's inner light. In therapy, it is important not to have to explain or control everything, nor overcome all difficulties or the symptoms being treated, because the therapist can never be certain to what extent the entirety of a patient's personality structure is held together by pathologic elements.

Occasionally, psychoanalysts speak of the absent self (Lesmeister 2009, 86f) when a feeling of being a nobody or a nothing prevails. Even successful people can be convinced that they are lacking identity and physical presence. Their inner world is often "desolate and empty" – corresponding to the negative pole of the mother archetype on a symbolical level. A young man from a very wealthy family with a university degree, an attractive girlfriend and a varied social life knows exactly how this feels. Nevertheless, he wants to undergo therapy because the inner boredom and emptiness he feels frighten him greatly. At best, such emptiness or nothingness ends up being a transit point, or dark creative place, a mother's womb out of which something new is born, according to German poet Goethe's famous saying "die and become". The images which conjure up such a place, also popular in psychotherapy for inspiring confidence, are the insides of a whale, a sea voyage by night or the underworld. We step down into the depths and come back renewed and revitalized – mortificatio is followed by rebirth. The journey into the underworld becomes the fountain of youth (Jung 1956, CW 5, §449).

In treating patients with early disturbances in this sphere of death, Margitta Giera-Krapp (Giera-Krapp 1988, 26ff) recommends adopting tempered aggressive behavior at the expense of a predominantly positive maternal attitude in therapy. Her patients found this approach was healing, as it facilitated an encounter at eye level, meaning that not only they, but also their counterpart was thought of as destructive. An emphatic, particularly protective, caring and nurturing maternal attitude often suppresses the transference that is necessary, i.e. mortificatio. Giera-Krapp describes the treatment of a 23-year-old man with a severe narcissistic disorder, whose aggression and hostility she first tried to counter with patience. Pretty soon she warded off his constant attempts to belittle her with ironic remarks, which on the one hand relieved her, but also made her feel guilty. This at the same time improved transference and countertransference.

Giera-Krapp also explains how risky it can be when the therapist sacrifices the ideal of a good mother, as for example in the treatment of a suicidal man. His attempts to threaten and denigrate her generated feelings of rage and resentment on her part. She could no longer and was no longer willing to play the motherly figure who carried him through and, despite his suicide threats, urged him to continue on his path alone or with the help of others. She was aware that her aggressive attitude could prove risky in the process and that she was pressuring her patient to take personal responsibility. The result was an improved therapeutic relationship, whereupon sessions could be continued on an altered basis.

Obviously, therapists who trust patients to deal with their aggression or anger in the best case mobilize the latter's resources and adult ego state. Giera-Krapp observed that patients with borderline and narcissistic personality disorders in particular have the tendency to yearn for an ideal mother figure, but at the same time have a need to destroy her. If therapists have internalized a therapeutic ideal of this kind, they must in turn sacrifice it in order not to fall victim to manipulation, denigration or helplessness. Sacrificing an ideal means giving up one's self-image, which is proof of control over oneself and the ability to endure fear.

If a sacrifice is made on a conscious level, it can help overcome stagnation, as in the example of a young teacher who felt she had not sufficiently recuperated during the summer holidays, and was not ready for the upcoming school year. Despite her tiredness, she had intended to use the last days of the holidays to prepare for classes and this weighed heavily upon her. She kept gnashing her teeth in her sleep, and one night, had the following dream: "I am by a river. A small boy is trying to catch a fish with his bare hands, but quickly catches a fat toad instead. The boy laughs happily, and the old man by his side joins in with his laughter. I am annoyed that I didn't manage to get a fish, and the toad is disgusting."

The dreamer was amazed at the high spirits and cheerfulness of the boy and the old man, which stood out in stark contrast to her angry dream self. The 6-year-old boy drew her attention to the past, as about six years prior to this, the dreamer had been on the verge of a breakdown, and had at that time taken radical steps in giving up her job and ending a difficult relationship. She had also moved houses and recovered quickly, both physically and mentally. Looking at her dream as a resource made it easier for her to accept the fact that her lost joy of living, and thus also energy and vitality, were hidden in unconscious masculine personality traits. It also involved accepting a disgusting fat toad, whose meaning had yet be discovered.

It should not be forgotten that dealing with the dark self also confronts us with what cannot be transformed or healed. In this context, Marie-Louise von Franz warns against letting a quantum of goodness lead us to hope. Should, for example, a person with a destructive nature have a soft spot in their soul, this does not justify sentimental feelings of pity, because this spot alone usually does not suffice as a source of good. It only serves to deceive and manipulate people even more. Von Franz is convinced that Hitler would not have become so dangerous if his statements had not occasionally been correct. National Socialism would hardly have become such a powerful force if an archetypal religious impulse had not triggered enthusiasm in some people for great deeds, emotions and the willingness to make sacrifices (von Franz 1997, 93f). It is exactly this good contained in evil which makes the latter so particularly dangerous and it should not be spared or nurtured. Such evil cannot be transformed, but must be stopped effectively or eradicated. We see this in fairy tales, for example in Grimm's fairy tale *Hänsel und Gretel*, in which Gretel kills the wicked witch without feeling any pity. This is not always easy to do, because it contradicts our ideal of being a good person.

Furthermore, the dark self confronts us with increasing destructiveness. In this regard, Hultberg mentions that in the 20th century, the most talented and creative people were silenced by fellow human beings or destructive political systems, which Hultberg again sees as an expression of the dark self, with the result that:

> The self turns against the self. By destroying the only possibility it has to manifest itself, the self erases itself, so to speak. We seem to be dealing here with a shocking and fundamental paradox that is typical of our time: the destructive aspect of the self has become self-destructive. The self annihilates the powers of the ego, but in this way, invalidates itself. (Hultberg 2009, 224 *)

Hultberg describes how interwoven the development of the ego and the self and their interrelationship are, in the sense that both the ego and the self need each other. Whoever destroys the ego, which can make the dark side of the self conscious, also destroys the self.

Banishing Evil? On Trending Taboos

In an article which appeared in *The Sydney Morning Herald* on 24 February 2017, Kasey Edwards described how she introduced a hard-and-fast rule to be observed by the family as of the birth of her first daughter. In future, no male, even relatives and friends, would be allowed to babysit the girl on their own. At a later date, out-of-school activities, such as basketball camps or holiday camps, where men have unrestricted and unsupervised access to children, became a taboo. Whenever her daughter would visit classmates or go to parties, she always ensured that a woman was present. The measures she took to protect her daughter were based on the widespread sexual abuse of girls by men.

Although not many parents resort to such drastic action, they are nowadays in general much more concerned about protecting children from harm and negative experiences from an early age on, in the belief that children should be allowed to grow up as carefree and happily as possible.

Some parents therefore also refuse to read fairy tales to their children, because they consider their themes too violent. This protective attitude continues into adulthood with students themselves requesting that they be warned if teaching materials contain traumatizing content. If, for example, Ovid's Metamorphoses are on the curriculum, professors are required to point out any passages containing scenes of violence, to allow students to leave the classroom in time. The university campus should be a safe place. Even if such demands are in part well-founded on a rational level, efforts to avoid any dark material is disadvantageous, since people lose out on the chance to increase their knowledge about and their ability to deal with the dark forces of destruction which these stories teach. Fairy tales and myths therefore foster a strong ego.

Furthermore, shielding or protecting one's offspring does not necessarily result in their having a bright and light psyche, because the dark self belongs to every human soul. Regina Renn (Renn 2012, 429ff) relates the story of a young woman who suffers from an anxiety disorder and is tormented by sadistic dreams, despite having very loving and caring parents. She also feels a boundless inner emptiness and that she is a nobody. In my opinion, such symptoms are not surprising and remind us of the fairy tale *Sleeping Beauty*. In the story, a child favored by fate is protected by a loving father who tries to remove any possible threats from his realm – which are symbolized by the spindles in the fairy tale. As a young girl, *Sleeping Beauty* meets an old woman with a spinning wheel, pricks her finger on the spindle and falls into her famous long sleep. The father's protection strategy thus remains unsuccessful.[14] *Sleeping Beauty* becomes motionless and drained of all emotion. Her sleep could be interpreted as a loss of vitality, as a severe depression, during which her ability to relate to others is also suspended.

Hence, it can indeed be fatal to withhold the dark self from people, as it is necessary for the development of human identity. Moreover, the dark self still remains, even if it is banished or avoided. It is therefore beneficial to relate to it and deal with it on a conscious level. Marie-Louise von Franz is convinced that this is the way to developing a philanthropic ego-identity, and forcing back egocentricity (von Franz 1993, 1).

---

14. I like to refer to Jeremiah Gotthelf's tale *The Black Spider*, where locking away was the right thing to do, which shows that there is no obvious right answer.

6. The Ego, the Self and Time

To Whom Does Time Belong?

There is a saying in German that refers to the departure from this life and literally translates to "blessing (our earthly) time" in English ("das Zeitliche segnen"). It originated in the 17th century, when it was customary to seek God's blessing for those about to become bereaved before one's death, since a good earthly life lay in God's hands according to the biblical psalm "My time is in your hands" (Psalm 31.15).

When close to death, people worry about the loved ones they are about to leave on earth, however, this is expressed in an increasing number of different ways. They wish to do something good for the living, therefore in obituaries we read that we should refrain from buying flowers or wreaths for the grave and donate money to a charity instead. What at first seems to be an altruistic need on the part of the deceased to accomplish something good and useful for the living may perhaps have other facets of meaning. The tradition of flower decorations on coffins could have originated because plant life points to the psychic mystery of death and resurrection. Plants draw their life directly from inorganic matter and refer us to the miracle of life which can arise from dead matter. The corpse of a human being consists solely of inorganic matter, and for Marie-Louise von Franz (Franz 1986, 38), the rich giving of flowers and wreaths at funerals was the unconscious expression of a belief in resurrection. Therefore, refraining from laying flowers at the grave could also be seen as an expression of dwindling belief in the immortality of the soul.

In comparison to the 17th century, earthly life is significantly less to be found in God's hands, whom we no longer need to ensure a qualitatively pleasing life in many areas. Even if the greater part of Germany's harvest were to be destroyed by thunderstorms, the population would not need to fear famine. There would still be plenty of food in the supermarkets and praying to God would not be necessary in such a situation, yet money would be needed because food would become more expensive. And as soon as we fall sick, we first hurry to the doctor and the pharmacy instead of praying. We even have less and less recourse to guardian angels for our children because the helmet law for cyclists, booster car seats and vaccinations considerably reduce these and many other life-threatening situations that might arise.

The ongoing process of overcoming natural dependencies includes the dependency on natural rhythmic time, to which regularly recurring phenomena such as day and night, the seasons, phases of the moon or the menstrual cycle belong. The periodic time of Mother Nature is symbolically seen as a feminine sensual time of death and birth. And if there is a female time, what would be the equivalent male time? Probably linearly clocked time, largely independent of natural rhythms, perfected for carrying out piecework on the assembly line, where time is divided into units of equal length and equal sequence in the interests of efficiency and profit. Humankind has succeeded in winning additional leeway within the limits of natural time, by urging us to abolish Sunday as a periodically recurring day of rest, by shifting the menstrual cycle or sleep/wake cycle with the help of medication, and then again making fruit available out-of-season. Perhaps we should not therefore speak of male time, but it would rather be more appropriate to speak of time used in a male fashion, since as long as we are alive on this earth, we will somehow never be able to shake off nature's rhythms.[15]

Observing the natural rhythm of time is not only outmoded, quasi antiquated, but also problematic from an economic point of view. If we did not yet have electricity to provide us with light, we would have to go to bed at sunset and get up at sunrise, as Paracelsus recommended in the 16th century. We would be dependent on natural sunlight to be productive. Then again, we would be able to sleep longer in winter than in summer due to our degree of latitude. But since nowadays both electricity and light are available around the clock, we can and must work at any time of day or night.

Quite unimaginable and no longer really comprehensible is the fact that during the Middle Ages, anyone who worked at night was thought to have been in league with death. Night, derived from the word "noceo" meaning shadow, was regarded to be the time of spirits, the restless dead and temptation by hostile, even diabolical powers, and so the city gates were closed. Sunrise was the only time for people to be up and about. With light, life began, analogous with the myths of

---

15. Our measurement of time has long since departed from that of natural timekeeping to the extent that we no longer use mountain peaks in the Alpine region such as the Neunerkofel, the Elferkofel, the Zwölferkofel or the Einserkofel, the Rocher du Midi or the Mittagshorn in Switzerland as sundials (*translator's note: the names of the mountains each refer to a particular time of day*). Yet, to this day, a naturally rhythmic process is still being used as a basis for timekeeping: the imperceptible oscillations in the cesium atom define the length of a second. More info: Geissler 2001, 35.

creation, which usually begin with the expulsion of darkness. In those days as well as in the Middle Ages, time belonged to God and it was therefore sinful to trade in it, as a medieval book for confessors explains:

> The usurer does not lend the debtor what is his, but only the time that belongs to God. Usurers are thieves, for they trade in time that does not belong to them. Moreover, since they trade in nothing but expected money, that is, time, they trade in days and nights. But the day is the time of brightness, and the night is the time of peaceful rest. Even when a usurer is asleep, his business goes on cheerfully, and he draws his profit from it. (Geissler 2001, 30, 36 *)

But in Christianity, time no longer belongs to God. By the 14th century, it had become a trade commodity after Pope John XXII – a strict opponent of the Franciscan ideal of poverty – lifted the ban on interest, thus laying the foundations for our money to continuously gain interest without us having to feel remorse. What was once considered a terrible sin is the engine of today's economy where real output is gambled on at least tenfold and the player archetype rules the world. Unimaginable sums are constantly being chased around the globe as virtual money streams, and fractions of a second can make all the difference to gigantic wins or losses. Infinitesimal, barely perceptible time advantages are significant, something which incidentally also applies to some sports.

The fact that time no longer belongs to God has not only financial, but also ethical consequences. Not only in the form of assisted suicide where the moment of death can be freely chosen, but also when dealing with the desynchronization of cultures, where significant time imbalance exists. An approximately 100-year wage differential between factory workers in Switzerland or Germany[16] and Bangladesh makes products manufactured in South Asia affordable to us and guarantees our current prosperity. And a desynchronization in the extraction of raw materials is impoverishing Mother Earth, since we are depleting oil and gas much faster than it can be renewed.

Quality and Demands of Time

The different ways in which time is used and the different time demands of children and adults can lead to major conflicts in daily life. Barbara Sichtermann (Geißler 1997, 120) refers to the perception of time in young children as anarchic and by this means the spontaneous and emotive way they deal with time. Basically, a young child demands us to take our time and dawdle. But adults do not have any time: they cannot pander to a child's anarchic time demands, but rather force them to adapt to the linear time structures of the adult world at an increasingly early age. In 2006, a guidebook advising parents how their child can be out of diapers, i.e. dry, between the age of 4-6 months apparently became a bestseller in the USA.

Early learning support programs are applied at a younger and younger age to prevent children from falling behind. Time is therefore organized and assigned from the very beginning and used in a disciplined manner to cater to the working environment. This leads to daily fights with children, which they cannot hope to win. In light of the ongoing discussion about the scarce places in day nurseries and the balancing of work and family life, the time demands of children are regularly suppressed and sacrificed in favor of economic structures. It

16. Textile workers in Bangladesh today earn less than 30 Euro, a German employee earned about 120 Euro per month in 1950.

is not only children who suffer, but also our ability to love, because relationships need time. The economy benefits from these changing needs of time, since it continues to succeed in channeling the emotions of people who no longer have time for relationships into the purchase of consumer goods as an alternative (Baumann 2009, 71).

It would be only too easy to rail against our modern time management because at least 1,500 years have elapsed since its invention. Benedict of Nursia (510-540) previously indicated that labor could make our earthly time of value, thus helping us to come closer to post-mortal salvation. For this to succeed, schedules needed to be drawn up in order to organize time for food, fasting, work, prayer and sleep. These kinds of schedules have been possible ever since people started leading future-oriented lives. The ability to postpone in favor of a future reward is an exclusively human ability. Only crows and ravens can be trained to curb their appetite for food for a maximum of five minutes, if they are then rewarded with food of a higher quality (Wittmann 2014, 11).

If we want to overcome natural time, we do not necessarily require discipline or a fight, but sometimes merely a lot of money, skills and cunning. Wealthy people no longer have to wait 30 or 50 years, which they might not have left to live anyway, for a magnificent park to thrive on their property. They can afford to purchase older trees[17] immediately and therefore save themselves the time that these would require to mature. The saying in German "You cannot transplant a mature tree" is outdated nowadays, both on the concrete and symbolic level. However, it must be noted that a mature tree can only be transplanted if a tree nursery replants it every three to five years and trims the crown in such a way that leaf mass and root ball achieve an optimum balance.

---

17. A 50-year old oak tree costs around 30 000 Euro.

Physical time is also purchasable nowadays. In our affluent Western world, women can keep the so-called ticking biological clock at bay, meaning the natural timespan for conception, by means of freezing egg cells (social freezing).[18] This in turn makes new forms of gifts possible, as there are parents who are willing to cover the costs of egg freezing. They therefore gift their daughter with an opportunity for late motherhood and themselves with the chance of becoming grandparents at some future point.

If time is purchasable, this makes it a tradable object: we can dispose of it, waste it or use it, gain it or save it. But time is not only an object. As soon as we speak about time flowing, passing or running, we perceive it as a subject, as something independent. And when time heals, it is not only a subject, but also has an effect. Regardless of whether object or subject, time can neither be seen nor heard – it is invisible and silent, but always present.

The examples cited above demonstrate that time, whatever that is, appears as a polarity in the Western world. This is again manifested in death: the idea of an immortal soul described by Plato and taken up in Christianity and other religions is based on a dualistic view of humanity, which implies two polar time qualities. Whereas the mortal body of humans only exists for a limited time period, the immortal soul is liberated in death and lives on in eternity. Death marks the threshold or break between finite and eternal time, between earthly life and a post-mortal life in the hereafter. Should therefore the belief in the afterlife of the soul dwindle – which appears to be indicated by the previously referred to renunciation of flowers at the grave, as well as surveys, or the neurobiological theory that the spirit and the soul are a by-product of nerve cells

---

18. Until now nature has only awarded men fertility into old age, but technology has come to ensure equal rights for men and women in this respect.

– then this would have a huge effect on our understanding as well as handling of time. Hereafter eternity is a place which humans have always filled with projected images. Eternity is thus an exemplary place in Christianity where God will compensate us for any injustice suffered in this world. The concept of the Last Judgement is highly relevant for believers, both perpetrators and victims. As a perpetrator, I know that I cannot escape punishment and atonement should I not be able to curb my potential evil nature, my shadow potential. And as a victim, I may trust that my earthly suffering will not only be seen, but also compensated for postmortem. Both worlds are intertwined, and between them, there are transfers and compensation payments. If there were no Last Judgement, I would never need to fear postmortem punishment and could live unrestrained and recklessly in this world. On the other hand, any scores left unsettled threaten to lapse in the afterlife. Injustice, corrupt power structures or outrageous grievances cannot be delegated to a higher power and be avenged after death. With the loss of the afterlife, any reckoning is only possible on earth.

If the afterlife and eternity are no longer options we believe in, then all our related projections will need to be withdrawn and the ensuing emotions and consequences somehow overcome. For example, the belief that rewards are to be expected in Paradise would be obsolete, even if we have led a diligent, godly life, as Benedict of Nursia hoped, or after we have committed a suicide bombing.

The withdrawal of such projections raises the question of the meaning of life anew. How can we bear the loss of eternity, i.e. the continuous life of the soul after death? If we do not feel emotionally and spiritually able to stand up to the consequences of a dwindling belief in the afterlife, if we do not find answers, many of us will remain inclined to suppress

139

death. But the need for eternity and eternal values is far from lost. Some people tend to compensate for this by finding eternity in earthly life. The watch industry, for example, promotes this longing by naming one of its watches *Eterna*. But in the end, eternity cannot be grasped in a material way.

Accelerated Life

For sociologist Hartmut Rosa, the longing for eternity is an additional motor to our acceleration efforts, and the cause of our highly accelerated lifestyle in comparison to the Middle Ages (Rosa 2005, 39). If life beyond death no longer beckons, then we are considerably restricted. Experience can only be gained in the very short lifespan of the here and now. Since our earthly lifespan has increased negligibly in comparison to universal time, and still defies a substantial increase in contrast to money, a faster and faster pace of life remains the only way forward for us. Only those who step on the accelerator can accommodate the most possible options before death. Whosoever lives twice as fast, saves half the usual time needed for each action and can double the sum of experience or activities. In accordance with the physical definition that performance is work per time, this means the faster we live, the more experience we can collect.

When Woody Allen was once asked what his thoughts about death were, he reportedly answered: "I am against it". People suffering from a grave illness will occasionally refute this statement, saying they await death as a deliverance. But those who lead a good, self-determined and fulfilled life, do not want it to end, especially if there is nothing to expect afterwards. In this respect, accelerating the pace of life could indeed be seen as an answer to the problem of our finiteness.

The finiteness of a life without an afterlife could have spurred our hunger, perhaps even greed for life. Whereas "real" famine, i.e., the lack of food, exists in the so-called developing countries, we in the Western world are suffering from "time famine". Hartmut Rosa explains why the possibilities open to us for acceleration cannot solve the problem of finiteness, but rather leave us frustrated, exhausted, maybe even desperate. The same techniques which help us to save time lead to an explosion of global options. Although we are becoming faster and faster – in the field of data transfer we have reached the speed of light and therefore maximum speed – the ratio between missed and realized options is steadily increasing. In other words, the liveable percentage of the cake of global options available to us is shrinking.

The Unlived Life

Some people's reaction to missed opportunities can border on panic and they repeatedly ask themselves: "Is that it?" For Thomas Fuchs (Fuchs 2008, 221ff), this is unlived life knocking at the door. In his psychiatric practice, he found out that the opportunities we left unfinished or missed in life tend to remain present and active in our minds. They can be recalled more easily and are commonly associated far more with regret than the opportunities we took. This could be a result of our ability to project far more positively onto the unlived, and the fact that these projections tend to be ideal and devoid of criticism. Missed opportunities in life can give rise to feelings of guilt and inadequacy, but also benefit us with a compelling desire to shape the future.

Unlived life does not only have to be based on fate or missed opportunities, but can also arise from inner reservations, which tempt us not to want anything definite. Our actions remain non-committal and this enables us to move forward quickly in favor of other possibilities. Jaspers calls this neurotic provisionality.

Alchemical symbolism interprets a lived life as a process of "Coagulatio", as becoming concrete through the element of earth (Edinger 1990, 109). In Coagulatio, something solidifies and thereby acquires form, shape and boundaries. Whosoever longs for a more fulfilled life needs the process of Coagulatio to realize creativity.

In psychotherapy, Coagulatio is promoted by an active, open-minded and participatory behavior on the part of the psychotherapist. Both the therapist and the patient promote Coagulatio by taking responsibility for personal fantasies and ideas, and expressing them or giving them shape by means of creative media. Numerous people suffering from anhedonia need Coagulatio, whereas the process is less helpful to people who are driven too strongly by desire or who are too materialistic in outlook.

Mental Illness as a Consequence of Modern Time Use

According to Jung, mental syndromes take up, compensate for and symbolize the collective problems of an era. This theory begs the question whether increases in depressive illnesses might be a consequence of unfulfilled acceleration demands. It is not difficult to recognize that any desire for acceleration fails during a depression or burn-out. In both illnesses, the ego or ego-complex are radically thwarted and the speed of lifetime achievement tends towards almost zero, as both depression and burn-out cause us to lose ourselves in time. Marc Wittmann speaks of the loss of the ego in such situations (Wittmann 2014, 132). Both illnesses force us not only to abandon the usual pace of social life, but also remind us of the wider polarity in the time we experience. Time is an externally measurable objective, as an hour is the same everywhere in the world for every living being. However, the inner experience of this equally long time period, i.e. the quality of time, is very different subjectively: time passes in a completely different way when we experience something good and are joyful and happy than when we are experiencing something terrible. We often experience minutes of terror or fear as a never-ending period of time, a small eternity.

Objective time measurement and our subjective perception of event duration always diverge considerably when we experience events following in rapid succession, or conversely experience emptiness or boredom. Moments of shock in life-threatening situations influence our subjective awareness of time. Subjectively, time appears to pass very slowly, creating an impression of slow-motion or even of time standing still. In contrast, days full of enriching encounters appear much shorter to the ego-consciousness than routine workdays devoid of emotionally touching experience.

The ego-consciousness and consciousness of time are thus inseparable. "No ego without time" and "I am time", states Marc Wittmann (Wittmann 2018). We seldom appreciate that time cannot be perceived by the senses. It is emotional experience that opens up the subjective flow of time to the ego. The way we experience time is inseparably connected with our physical experiences, as proven by psychological and neurobiological studies over the past ten years. In 1905, French psychiatrist Gabriel Revault d'Allones (Wittman 2015, 83) described a 53-year old patient who experienced neither hunger nor satiety. She ate because she knew how much a person should eat. She experienced neither tiredness nor a feeling of having had enough sleep. Ice cold or hot water made no difference to her, but feelings such as sadness and joy had also become foreign. At the beginning of her disorder, the patient had completely lost all subjective sense of time and could no longer judge whether a few seconds or hours had elapsed without a clock.

Neuro-physiologically speaking, time perception processes take place in the sunken part of the cerebral cortex, the so-called insular cortex. Marc Wittmann's research into functional magnetic resonance imagery at the University of San Diego in California indicated that time progression and duration are encoded in the insular cortex as an increase in body signals. Physical sensations, such as temperature, pain and touch, as well as information from the inner organs flow through the insulae, arousing emotions and evoking a sense of time. Neurological research into epilepsy, especially the ecstatic auras – such as those also experienced by Fyodor Dostoevsky – has demonstrated that the ego experiences an exciting feeling of presence, accompanied by an increase of activity in the insular cortex. People who have experience in meditation and who therefore have long years of practicing this feeling of presence and time expansion, increase their insula grey matter volume (Wittmann 2015, 94, 99, 100).

The so-called subjective time paradox also belongs to the measurement of time by the ego-complex which states that experienced and remembered time are inversely proportional to each other. Stimulating, exciting days are usually diverting, but appear long in retrospect. Boring, frustrating hours run slowly and tenaciously, but are remembered as being short. Time shrinks in memory in accordance with the motto: where did the whole of Sunday go to? How could the day fly past so quickly, although we did not do or experience anything of note? The impression remains that the day passed like nothing as if by magic. This typical time paradox between experience and memory results in a perceived short/long time ratio and vice versa.

According to Hartmut Rosa, we are increasingly confronted by short/short patterns in our accelerated society, where we acquire lots of experience, but little of this is impressive. However, exactly this is relevant, as it shapes and touches individuals emotionally and will not be forgotten. It leaves traces in such a lasting way that we hardly need souvenirs or photos (Rosa 2013a, 136ff). Back in 1954, psychiatrist Victor von Gebsattel drew our attention to the fact that the normal course of experiencing time is distorted during periods of deep depression. Transcultural studies (Hell 2000, 41) indicate a similar core area in experiencing depression across cultures. This shared core symptomatology corresponds to a feeling of inhibition and the impression of slowing down. People suffering from depression stress "how slowly time passes", the deeper their depression becomes. Some people perceive time as standing still: "I no longer have a sense of time, my inner clock seems to be at a standstill, whereas the timeclock appears to continue to run for others. I don't seem to be making any progress in anything I do. I feel paralyzed, unable to move forward". In his diaries, Kierkegaard writes of the feeling of not moving from the spot as a phenomenon of "time halted". Time coagulates to something that has been, to something decaying. The past catches up with us. According to time estimation studies, severely depressed patients perceive a period of time ahead of them as being much shorter than healthy people. They believe that their future holds less time, while simultaneously, already elapsed time appears to be longer in retrospect than it was in reality, which makes the past seem overpowering (Hell 2000, 52f).

People suffering from ADS or other impulse control disorders also display abnormalities in their perception of time. They perceive seconds and minutes as being much longer than people without this disorder. Many parents recognize that healthy children also have difficulty waiting and repeatedly ask: "How much longer is it going to take?", because they have not yet learnt to estimate amounts of time and are therefore less patient than most adults (Wittmann 2018). Yet exactly this inability to perceive time realistically also has its advantages, as it allows them to be fun-loving, spontaneous and to live for the moment.

We cannot, in my opinion, fully escape the collective acceleration process. Efficient time management is not an appropriate method for sustainable deceleration and a healthy slower pace of life, because it remains within the parameters of linear temporal logic. This is how I see it because acceleration happens not only to humans, but affects the whole cosmos and is therefore probably an archetypal phenomenon, the background to which we do not understand. In 2011, three cosmologists from Australia and the USA, who made up part of the teams surrounding Saul Perlmutter as well as Brian P. Schmidt and Adam G. Riess, were awarded the Nobel Prize for Physics after their discovery of the accelerated rate of expansion of the universe in 1998 (Bührke 2011). They demonstrated that matter actually slowed down the expansion of space until about halfway through the present age, as is generally assumed, but then acceleration set in and the universe has been expanding at an increasing rate ever since. This behavior is caused by so-called Dark Energy, which is driving the universe apart like steam in a pressure cooker.

Interestingly enough, this discovery was made shortly before the millennium, almost at the same time as the speed-of-light was reached in communications which we all use today when sending emails, text messages, skyping or surfing the internet. But, even if the theory that acceleration is an archetype encompassing all life's realities holds true, this should not make us fatalistic. Charlie Chaplin's Film *Modern Times* dating back to 1936 could demonstrate in which direction acceleration should and could lead us. The first interim title in *Modern Times* describes the story of diligence, entrepreneurial spirit, open competition and humanity's quest for happiness – clearly a highly topical subject even 80 years after the premiere. The opening scene shows a clock whose hands indicate the time as two minutes before six. A throng of workers are hurrying to the factory, one of them being the assembly line worker Charlie (Chaplin). The steadily increasing speed of piecework results in Charlie developing motoric twitches. The unreasonable demands of this piecework finally land him in a mental asylum. His ego is no match for the strain of this time structure.

The film demonstrates how technology dictates our time. How we master time has migrated and can be observed against the backdrop of the concepts of ego and self. Originally belonging to God, this time mastery gradually fell under the control of the ego, only to be lost again to us because of technical progress and acceleration in many spheres of life. We can see this migration if we look at nuclear power where secure storage sites are needed for unimaginably long periods of time. We have brought eternity to earth with our nuclear waste, in a manner of speaking, because we need it to render this waste harmless. This and other human-made technologies are beginning to burden us in an unprecedented manner and deprive us of our room to maneuver.

In the final scene of *Modern Times,* we see the worker Charlie and his girlfriend walk down the street towards sunrise. If we were to interpret this ending similarly to the end of a fairy tale, then relationships would be the solution to the dilemma of time. The relationship between male and female enables us to deal with time pressure. The feminine has to be rediscovered and the relationship with the feminine has to be cultivated, because by means of a healthy relationship with our bodies, cyclical nature, the emotions, feelings and love, we are able to stop the rush of performance, efficiency and speed which has its hold on us. Emotions are essentially slow and those who allow feelings, take their time and lay the groundwork for a fertile connection between female and male time. And this is not a regression, not a longing for the good old days, when everything was better.

Eternity

What exactly is eternity? One definition says that eternity is something with neither beginning nor end which exists independently of the phenomenon of time. This is time-lessness: something unimaginable, but according to French philosopher and sinologist François Jullien, something self-evident. In his book *The Silent Transformations* (Jullien, 2011), he draws attention to the completely different Western and Eastern concepts of time. The Greek tradition since Plato and Aristotle thinks in terms of being and substance. Logos defines things, identifies, orders, separates, and catalogues. A is A and A is not equal to B. Logos draws boundaries between things and properties, aims at clarity, freedom from contra-diction and, according to Jullien, is not able to conceptualize snow that is just melting. That is to say, as soon as snow melts, it is no longer definable.

Chinese thinking directs its attention precisely to this transition, and thus to the point where Greek thinking falters.

The Chinese view, according to Jullien, is not that of essence and identification, but rather that of energy flowing in the constant change of things (Jullien, 2011). This change has neither beginning nor end, i.e. eternal character, and prevents us from determining where one characteristic or quality ends and where the next begins. This view of change cannot draw on affiliations, as the view of the category of being must inevitably do. Transformation constantly dissolves, is a game of polarities, where the evolvement of the one is necessarily accompanied by the shrinking of the other.

This is reminiscent of a lecture by Hartmut Rosa in April 2013, in which he described the individual and ego-experience in the context of changing time relations: In pre-modern times, it was clear who I was. Birth decided my destiny and my place in the hierarchy, which as a sacred, predetermined order was irrevocable with only little leeway for the individual. In modernity, the question arose: Who am I? Identity was no longer fixed, but was allowed, indeed had to be sought and found. The goal was to find one's place and position and form a stable identity in a stable environment, which also includes what is called individuation – the task of finding one's own destiny in relation to the self.

According to Rosa, this path is outdated in the current post- or late modern age, where stable identity is replaced by performative identity. It is no longer about finding one's place, but avoiding taking positions. So-called surfers (riding the wave) or drifters (getting thrown back and forth) and their ability to adapt to permanent movements are in demand. Our desire for inner and external stability could be overridden, and in addition, the pace at which the demand for change hits us seems overwhelming. In view of this quality of time, individuals today seem to be forced to keep their egos in a constant state of flux, which in the view of the ancient alchemists corresponds to the process of Solutio. According to Zygmunt Baumann, the experience of increased disconnection and incompletion shows that we have left both cyclical and linear time behind and have arrived at a time of pointillism and fracture – characterized by discontinuity, inconsistency and a lack of cohesion. Our own life splinters or fragments because experiences become akin to individual, disconnected dots (Baumann 2009, 46). At best, it is possible to recognize meaningful patterns in retrospect. Lesmeister employs the images of the fragmented person, the patchwork identity, as well as the vagabond or tourist identity to describe such ego states (Lesmeister 2009, 26 ff).

These observations are not entirely new. Back in the 18th century, Scottish philosopher David Hume (1711-1776) stated that his ego was not to be found in a bundle of perceptions. For him, the ego was not a thing or an object, but a procedure, a constitutive process, more subjective rather than subject (Wittmann, 2018). This coincides with C.G. Jung's view of the ego-complex not as a fully formed, stable-static entity, comparable to all other complexes, but as a lifelong, dynamic process of development. Today, however, the collective process would appear to emphasize dynamics at the expense of stability, which is why the motto "Become who you are" is increasingly less valid than "Be who you become".

Other time structures are in flux, and more recently, it is not so much punctuality, but rather flexibility that is held as a virtue. Where people are based and where they work is no longer of such importance as their accessibility. And because of this disregard for cyclical time requirements, many people are expected to be available at any time of night or day.

Can the Chinese viewpoint, introduced by Jullien above, also be applied when it comes to birth and death, the beginning and the end of being? The beginning of every life means the transformation of something fleeting and intangible into breath, the breath into form, the form into life (Jullien 2011). This concept does not view being as a break from what came previously, rather as a transition of the invisible to the visible. And death is not an event falling outside the boundaries, as foreseen in Western philosophy. François Jullien confronts us with the question:

> Have we not therefore erected time as a total subject, easily assignable and therefore conveniently invocable because, for want of according a sufficient status to silent transformations, we needed to invoke a great agent to account at the same time for the emergence of things into the visible and for their invisible reabsorption. (Jullien 2011, 110f)

He postulates that time is a construction invented by the European language and that it mostly leads us astray.

In search of an answer to this theory, it might be worth revisiting the era when the German phrase about "blessing our earthly time" was coined. It was during this time that the deeply religious Isaac Newton lived. In 1687, he presented his closed physical theory which was the first act since the Creation not to require divine intervention. Time which flows without relation to an external object forms the backdrop to his equations of motion of matter through space. According to Newton, the time t exists of itself, independently of what happens in time. It is absolute and external, and something in which we swim so to speak. Physics professor Wolfram Schommers (Schommers 1997, 88) points out that although Newton's idea is well suited to the human perception of time in terms of flow, it is by no means plausible in other respects. For example, what should this sea of time consist of? A verifiable time substrate would have to exist and somebody or something would have to somehow create time. There is no evidence for all this so far. Irreversible processes, such as a cooling cup of coffee, evolution or aging, in particular, lead us to conclude that a connection between time and process must exist. This viewpoint leads directly to the concept of system-specific, inner time. Time should therefore be defined by the process itself that is to be examined. According to Wolfram Schommers, time exists in our minds only. Here, he reconnects to Chinese thinking that does not share our idea of external time in the face of silent transformation. This also fits in with Marc Wittmann's previously mentioned theory: "No ego without time" and "I am time".

Our Western thinking has not really come to grips with the nature of time. Time remains mysterious and is far from being what the clock measures. Albert Einstein discovered that clocks do not tick at the same speed everywhere. The faster a clock is carried from one place to another and the more the gravitational force increases, the slower the clock runs. Time and space are closely linked, and although these time phenomena can be observed in the cosmos, they hardly play a role in our "slow" everyday lives. However, the connection between space and time is eminently important for cultural life, as the phenomena of the finiteness of this world and eternity beyond show. According to cultural theologian Jean-Pierre Wils (Wils 2013, 37f), the way we experience space was a dominant factor of the so-called culture of presence, which was prevalent in the Middle Ages and which we have long since overcome. Life and religion were experienced physically and spatially in those days. The concrete took precedence over the abstract and space took precedence over time. However, space was by no means an empty container, but rather a sacred, energetically charged place. Religion was, as already mentioned, a materially-sensual experience, the touching of objects thought of as mysterious and powerful and the world inhabited by divine as well as diabolical beings: this was the world of symbolic realism. Matter and God-given meaning were inseparably connected. According to Jean-Pierre Wils, this sensual sphere in religion, experienced as a sense of presence, has been lost for at least the past 200 years.

It was first and foremost the acceleration dynamics of modernity which weakened this dominance of space: one could say that we left space far behind us. When we phone or skype, place and distance no longer play a role. Once space had been overcome, time, the shape of the future, reflection and abstraction all moved to the forefront of cultural self-understanding. This also meant that a view was dismissed that could not and did not yet have to separate appearance from significance, and sensual surface from deeper meaning: the owl was once Athena and not just the symbol of Athena. The latter still holds true today; meaning is no longer present on the surface, but hidden behind appearances, in the depths, which we are forced to penetrate in order to understand and hermeneutically interpret. Meaning can no longer be experienced or show itself directly and concretely, but must be sought.

Interestingly enough, people who, because of our accelerated society, have pushed themselves to their personal limits, or are stressed out or bored, have recently begun to practice mindfulness, thus withdrawing into presence, into the body, into sensuality and the space that we largely left behind and overcame. It seems as if we want and need no longer to neglect, but rather rediscover the body, and thus also female time and the present, instead of speculating primarily on the future. People who redirect their attention to the "here and now" to avoid their minds from wandering, by, for example, consciously inhaling and exhaling during mindfulness meditations, experience increased presence and body awareness and, as a result, time expansion. Marc Wittmann points to a way out for people for whom life and time seem to pass ever more quickly because of these phenomena: The richer, the more emotionally colored and varied our life experience is, the longer our lifetime will become subjectively speaking (Wittmann 2015, 105).

Let us return again to the phenomenon of eternity, which is not to be understood as an infinite duration of time, but as timelessness, and thus as the suspension of time. Following 35 years' or the equivalent of more than 50,000 hours' experience of spiritual meditation, Tilman Lhündrup Borghardt explains that the path to a feeling of timelessness is by concentrating on the here and now:

In a mystical experience, whether through meditation or drug intoxication, the ego is one with the world and often feels a sense of liberation and complete peace of mind. The ego witnesses what is happening as an observer, including movement and time. Both time and the ego exist. In this peaceful and relaxed state of absolute presence, the ego feels a sense of unity and is one with the world. The experience is completely different during "awakening", the highest level of spiritual meditation, when the duality of subject and object vanishes and egolessness and timelessness begin to emerge (Wittmann, 2015, 74ff).

Tilman Lhündrup Borghardt emphasizes that the recognition and description of this situation is only possible in retrospect, because the re-emerging ego is needed, and he goes on to add that words can hardly explain the experience of this awakening. It is a timeless awareness without beginning or end, an immersion into being, which cannot be compared or controlled, without a before or an after, without ego-feeling. The experience thus confirms the hypothesis made by Schommers and Wittmann.

From the viewpoint of Analytical Psychology, one could say that time only begins to exist once the ego-complex is present as a conscious observer. The awakening described by Tilman Lhündrup Borghardt can be understood as the voluntary immersion of the ego in the self, and the disappearance of the ego in the space-time continuum.

Afterword

Apparently, some of the developments described in this book have already been in the air since 1880. Fyodor Dostoevsky opened up for discussion the consequences of the loss of God in his novel *The Brothers Karamasov:* if we lose faith in the immortality of the soul, then not only love, but all the strength required to continue this earthly life will desert us. No more feelings of shame will exist, everything will be permitted, even cannibalism. On the other hand, if God ceased to exist, then human beings would rule the earth and that would be great. Chemistry would take the place of God – which we can narrow down further in the present day to neurobiology and neurochemistry.

Dostoevsky goes on to say that without God, egoism will be the rule of the day and people will take from life all that it has to offer to achieve happiness and luck (Dostoevsky 2002).

This and other facets of the self which have been presented – regardless of whether consciously perceived or not – influence therapeutic work. The Greek word "therapeuein" (healing) is indicative here as its original meaning was "to serve the gods" (Edinger 1990, 12). In psychology, therapy is formulated as dealing with the relationship between the ego and the self. This viewpoint sometimes falls on deaf ears nowadays. Eckhard Frick (Frick 2016, 479f) therefore points out that the Austrian guidelines for psychotherapy prohibit the active introduction of the themes of religion, prayer or spiritual ritual into therapy, as this is thought of as unethical. Accordingly, the self would appear to not only arouse occasional discomfort, but rather to remain a question of morals and taboo to this day. To this extent, the topic selected as well as the content I chose to write about is delicate.

However, in a few decades or centuries, people will probably look back on our age and say: "Oh, that was treated as something holy which could not be called into question in those days, this was a taboo and that was a dogma." Some of this will scarcely cause raised tempers anymore or may even have become meaningless. The self will reveal itself in other images and processes.

I would be happy if this book were to awaken the reader's curiosity about the topic and promote the ongoing discussions around it. At this point, I would like to express my thanks to all those who have supported me directly or indirectly in writing it.

Literature

Alvarez, Alfred. *The Savage God. A Study of Suicide.* New York: W.W. Norton & Company, 1990.

Arendt, Hannah. *Some Questions of Moral Philosophy.* In: Responsibility and Judgment. New York: Schocken, 2003.

Ariès, Philippe. *The Hour of our Death.* New York, Vintage Books, 2013.

Astor, Maggie. *Microchip implants for employees? One company says yes.* The New York Times, 25 July 2017. www.nytimes.com/2017/07/25/technology/microchips-wisconsin-company-employees.html.

Bauman, Zygmunt. *Consuming Life.* Cambridge: Polity Press, 2007.

Bernhard, Thomas. *Walking.* Chicago: The University of Chicago Press, 2003.

Bovensiepen, Gustav. *Leben in der Seifenblase. Entwicklungszusammenbruch und Verteidigung des Selbst in der Post-Adoleszenz.* In: Analytische Psychologie, 156. Frankfurt: Brandes & Apsel, 2009.

Brauchen wir Gott? Von der Suche nach dem ganz persönlichen Glauben. GEO Magazine, 01/2015.

Brothers Grimm. *Grimm's Fairytales. Forty-two Household Tales.* London: Forgotten Books, 2020.

Bührke, Thomas. *Physik-Nobelpreis: Das beschleunigte Universum.* Spektrum. de, 2011. www.spektrum.de/alias/nobelpreise-2011/physik-nobelpreis-das-beschleunigte-universum/1124738. Last accessed on 10 May 2020.

Damasio, Antonio. *The Feeling of what Happens. Body, Emotion and the Making of Consciousness.* London: Vintage Books, 2000.

Daniel, Renate. *Vom Spinnen, Weben und Vernetzen der Schicksalsfäden.* In: Kast, Verena (ed.) Aus reichen Quellen schöpfen. Ostfildern: Patmos, 2015.

Debarque, Lucas. Interview in *Kulturzeit.* 3sat, 7 April 2016.

Dostoevsky, Fyodor. *The Brothers Karamazov.* New York: Farrar, Straus and Giroux, 2002.

Deutsche Presse Agentur (dpa). *Schlank an die Macht: Junge Wähler mögen "Slim-Fit-Warrior".* Süddeutsche Zeitung, 2017.

Edinger, Edward F. *Der Weg der Seele. Der psychotherapeutische Prozess im Spiegel der Alchemie.* Munich: Kösel, 1990.

Edwards, Kasey. *Why I won't let any male babysit my children.* The Sydney Morning Herald. 24 February 2017. www.smh.com.au/lifestyle/why-i-wont-let-any-male-babysit-my-children-20170223-gujn4f.html. Last accessed on 22 May 2020.

Eggers, Dave. *The Circle.* New York: Vintage Books, 2013.

Microchip Implants for Employees? One Company Says Yes. The New York Times, 25 July 2017. www.nytimes.com/2017/07/25/technology/microchips-wisconsin-company-employees.html. Last accessed on 8 June 2020.

Evans, Stephen. *South Korea provokes teenage smartphone privacy row.* BBC Online. www.bbc.com/news/technology-33091990. Last accessed on 22 May 2020.

Flaßpöhler, Svenja. *Mein Wille geschehe. Sterben in Zeiten der Freitodhilfe.* Berlin: wjs, 2007.

Frick, Eckhard & von Peinen, Brigitte. *Gott in der Analytischen Situation.* Analytische Psychologie, 186. Frankfurt: Brandes & Apsel, 2016.

Fuchs, Thomas. *Leib und Lebenswelt. Neue philosophisch-psychiatrische Essays.* Zug: Prof. Dr. Alfred Schmid Stiftung, 2008.

Geißler, Karlheinz. *Es muss in diesem Leben mehr als Eile geben.* Freiburg: Herder, 1997.

Geißler, Karlheinz. *Vom Tempo der Welt. Am Ende der Uhrzeit.* Freiburg: Herder, 2001.

Giegerich, Wolfgang. *Die Atombombe als seelische Wirklichkeit. Versuch über den Geist des christlichen Abendlandes.* Zurich: Schweizer Spiegel Verlag, 1988.

Giera-Krapp, Margitta. *Konstellation des gut-bösen Mutterarchetyps bei der Behandlung früher Störungen.* Analytische Psychologie, 19. Frankfurt: Brandes & Apsel, 1988.

Gotthelf, Jeremias. *The Black Spider.* Richmond: Oneworld Classics, 2009.

Graf, Friedrich Wilhelm. *Missbrauchte Götter. Zum Menschenbilderstreit in der Moderne.* Munich: C.H. Beck, 2009.

Grünberg, Arnon. *Gnadenfrist.* Zurich: Diogenes, 2006.

Heiler, Friedrich. *Erscheinungsformen und Wesen der Religionen.* Stuttgart: Kohlhammer, 1979.

Hell, Daniel. *Welchen Sinn macht Depression?* Reinbek: Rowohlt, 2000.

Hollersen, Wiebke. *Das Gesetz der Anziehung*. Welt am Sonntag, 16 November 2014. www.welt.de/print/wams/wissen/article134380111/ Die-Gesetze-der-Anziehung.html. Last accessed on 11 April 2020.

Huf, Hans-Christian. *Die Geschichte der Schönheit*. Munich: Heyne, 2013.

Hultberg, Peer. *Zentrum und Umkreis: Die Rolle von Jungs Selbstbegriff in der Gegenwart*. In: Analytische Psychologie, 156 Frankfurt: Brandes & Apsel, 2009.

Jacobsohn, Helmuth & von Franz, Marie-Louise & Hurwitz, Sigmund. *Studies in Jungian Thought. Timeless Documents of the Soul*. Evanston: Northwestern University Press, 1968.

James, Erika Leonard. *Fifty Shades of Grey*. New York: Vintage Books, 2011.

Jullien, François. *The Silent Transformations*. Chicago: University of Chicago Press, 2011.

Jung, Carl Gustav. *Collected Works. Volume 5*. Princeton: Princeton University Press, 1956.

Jung, Carl Gustav. *Collected Works. Volume 11*. Princeton: Princeton University Press, 1958.

Jung, Carl Gustav. *Collected Works. Volume 9/1*. Princeton: Princeton University Press, 1959.

Jung, Carl Gustav. *Collected Works. Volume 9/2*. Princeton: Princeton University Press, 1959.

Jung, Carl Gustav. *Collected Works. Volume 3*. Princeton: Princeton University Press, 1960.

Jung, Carl Gustav. *Collected Works. Volume 7*. Princeton: Princeton University Press, 1966.

Jung, Carl Gustav. *Collected works. Volume 13*. Princeton: Princeton University Press, 1967.

Jung, Carl Gustav. *Collected Works. Volume 12*. Princeton: Princeton University Press, 1968.

Jung, Carl Gustav. *Collected Works. Volume 8*. Princeton: Princeton University Press, 1969.

Jung, Carl Gustav. *Collected Works. Volume 14/1*. Princeton: Princeton University Press, 1970.

Jung, Carl Gustav. *Collected Works. Volume 6*. Princeton: Princeton University Press, 1971.

Kant, Immanuel. *Critique of Practical Reason*. Cambridge: Cambridge University Press, 2015.

Kullmann, Kerstin. *Kampfauftrag Kind*. In: Spiegel Magazine 33/2013 magazin.spiegel.de/SP/2013/33/106677646/index.html. Last accessed on 11 April 2020.

Knobbe, Martin & Schmalenberg, Detlef. *Der Kannibale*. In: Stern, 31. 24 July 2003.

Lauer, Céline. *Der inszenierte Makel*. Welt am Sonntag, No. 13, 29 March 2015. www.welt.de/print/wams/debatte/article138885420/Der-inszenierte-Makel.html. Last accessed on 8 June 2020.

Lafontaine, Celine. *Die Postmortale Gesellschaft*. Wiesbaden: VS Verlag für Sozialwissenschaften, 2010.

Lesmeister, Roman. *Selbst und Individuation. Facetten von Subjektivität und Intersubjektivität in der Psychoanalyse*. Frankfurt: Brandes & Apsel, 2009.

Liessmann, Konrad Paul. *Schönheit*. Vienna: Facultas, 2009.

Lorenz, Konrad. *On Aggression*. London: Methuen & Co. Ltd, 1966.

Marquard, Odo. *In Defense of the Accidental. Philosophical studies*. Oxford: Oxford University Press, 1991.

Meister, Martina. *Es gibt keine Schönheit*. 2006. www.spiegel.de/spiegel/spiegelwissen/d-107233201.html. Last accessed on 9 April 2020.

Neimann, Susan. *Evil in Modern Thought. An Alternative History of Philosophy*. Princeton: Princeton University Press, 2004.

Neumann, Erich. *Amor and Psyche. The Psychic Development of the Feminine. A Commentary on the Tale by Apuleius*. Princeton: Princeton University Press, 1956.

O'Kane, Françoise. *Das dunkle Gesicht der Psyche*. In: Gorgo – Zeitschrift für archetypische Psychologie und bildhaftes Denken, 25. Zurich: Schweizer Spiegel Verlag, 1993

Orbach, Susie. *Bodies*. London: Profile Books, 2009.

Orwell, George. *1984*. London: Penguin Books, 1954.

Putsch, Christian. *Schönheit aus dem Schatten*. Welt am Sonntag No. 28, 12 July 2015. www.welt.de/vermischtes/article144027164/Fuer-die-Nachbarskinder-war-Thando-Hopa-die-Verfluchte.html. Last accessed on 18 May 2020.

Rilke, Rainer Maria. *Duino Elegies & The Sonnets to Orpheus*. New York: Vintage, 2009.

Renn, Regina. *Von der Vergötterung des Selbst und der Verteufelung des Ich*. In: Analytische Psychologie, 170, Frankfurt: Brandes & Apsel, 2012.

Rosa, Hartmut. *Beschleunigung. Die Veränderung der Zeitstrukturen in der Moderne*. Frankfurt/M: Suhrkamp, 2005.

Rosa, Hartmut. *Beschleunigung und Entfremdung*. Frankfurt: Suhrkamp, 2013a.

Rosa, Hartmut. *Neue Verunsicherungen – alte Ängste?* Opening lecture of the Lindau Psychotherapy Weeks on 14 April 2013.

Röser, Johannes. *Ich, das Gehirn und Gott*. In: Michael Ebertz und Meinhard Schmidt-Degenhard (eds.). *Was glauben die Hessen? Horizonte religiösen Lebens*. Berlin: LIT, 2014.

Roth, Gerhard. *Fühlen, Denken, Handeln. Wie das Gehirn unser Verhalten steuert*. Frankfurt: Suhrkamp, 2001.

Schommers, Wolfgang. *Zeit und Realität. Physikalische Ansätze – Philosophische Aspekte*. Zug: Prof. Dr. Alfred Schmid Stiftung, 1997.

Silesius, Angelus. *The Cherubinic Wanderer* (Classics of Western Spirituality Series), transl. by Maria Shrady. Mahwah: Paulist Press, 1986.

Solms, Marc, and Oliver Turnbull. *The Brain and the Inner World: An Introduction to the Neuroscience of the Subjective Experience*. New York: Other Press, 2004.

Steiner, John. *Psychic Retreats. Pathological Organizations in Psychotic, Neurotic and Borderline Patients*. London/New York: Routledge, 2003.

Teller, Janne. *Alles – worum es geht*. Munich: Carl Hanser Verlag, 2013.

Teller, Janne. *Nothing*. New York: Atheneum Books for Young Readers, 2010.

Vidal-Folch, Ignacio. *Tschernobyl? Auschwitz? Sichuan? Buchen Sie jetzt!* In: Welt am Sonntag, 23 August 2015. www.welt.de/reise/article145494029/Tschernobyl-Auschwitz-Sichuan-Buchen-Sie-jetzt.html. Last accessed on 21 April 2020. The article is based on the book by Ambroise Tézenas. *Tourisme de la désolation*. Paris: Actes Sud, 2014.

Vonessen, Franz. *Das kleine Welttheater. Das Märchen und die Philosophie*. Zug: Prof. Dr. Alfred Schmid-Stiftung, 1998.

von Franz, Marie-Louise. *Projection and Re-Collection in Jungian Psychology. Reflections of the Soul*. Chicago: Open Court Publishing, 1985.

von Franz, Marie-Louise. *On Dreams and Death. A Jungian Interpretation*. Boston: Shambhala, 1986.

von Franz, Marie-Louise. *Individuation in Fairy Tales*. Boston: Shambhala, 1990.

von Franz, Marie-Louise. *Psychotherapy*. Boston: Shambala, 1993.

von Franz, Marie-Louise. *Archetypal Dimensions of the Psyche*. Boston: Shambala, 1997.

von Franz, Marie-Louise. *The Cat. A Tale of Feminine Redemption*. Toronto: Inner City Books, 2000.

von Matt, Peter. *Öffentliche Verehrung der Luftgeister. Reden zur Literatur*. Munich: Hanser, 2003.

Vorkoeper, Ute. *Der Zwang der Freiheit*. ZEIT Online, 24 February 2006. www.zeit.de/feuilleton/kunst_naechste_generation/tod_3. Last accessed on 20 April 2020.

Walser, Martin. *Ein sterbender Mann*. Reinbek: Rowohlt, 2016.

Wehowsky, Stephan. *Grenzüberschreitungen. Zur Zukunft einer Gesellschaft im Labor*. In: Traute Schroeder-Kurth & Stephan Wehowsky (ed.). Das manipulierte Schicksal. Künstliche Befruchtung, Embryotransfer und pränatale Diagnostik. Frankfurt: J. Schweitzer, 1988.

Weinreb, Friedrich. *Gotteserfahrung*. Weiler: Thauros, 2002.

Whitmont, Edward. *The Alchemy of Healing*. Berkeley: North Atlantic Books, 1996.

Willemsen, Roger. *Wer wir waren. Zukunftsrede*. Frankfurt: S. Fischer, 2016.

Wils, Jean-Pierre. *Blasphemie. Erinnerungen an eine Zeit, als Religion noch Nervensache war*. In: Laubach, Thomas (ed.). Kann man Gott beleidigen? Zur aktuellen Blasphemie-Debatte. Freiburg: Herder, 2013.

Wittmann, Marc. *Altered States of Consciousness. Experiences out of Time and Self*. Cambridge: The MIT Press, 2018.

Wittmann, Marc. *Wenn die Zeit stehenbleibt. Kleine Psychologie der Grenzerfahrungen*. Munich: C.H. Beck, 2015.

List of Films

My Sister's Keeper. Warner Brothers, 2009. Based on the novel of the same name by Jodi Picoult. Director: Nick Cassavetes; screenplay by Jeremy Leven & Nick Cassavetes.

Emmas Glück. Pandora Film, 2007. Based on the novel of the same name by Claudia Schreiber. Director: Sven Taddicken; screenplay by Ruth Thoma & Claudia Schreiber.

In Time. Twentieth Century Fox, 2011. Director and screenplay: Andrew Niccol.

Modern Times. United Artists, 1936. Director and screenplay: Charlie Chaplin.

Terror – Ihr Urteil. Constantin Film, 2016. Director: Lars Kraume; screenplay: Ferdinand von Schirach.

English Titles from Daimon

Our books are available from your bookstore or from our distributors:

Baker & Taylor	Gazelle Book Services Ltd.
30 Amberwood Parkway	White Cross Mills, High Town
Ashland OH 44805, USA	Lancaster LA1 4XS, UK
Phone: 419-281-5100	Tel: +44 1524 528500
Fax: 419-281-0200	Email: sales@gazellebookservices.co.uk
www.btpubservices.com	www.gazellebookservices.co.uk

Daimon Verlag - Hauptstrasse 85 - CH-8840 Einsiedeln - Switzerland
Phone: (41)(55) 412 2266
Email: info@daimon.ch
Visit our website: **www.daimon.ch** or write for our complete catalog